What the New Breed of CMOs Know That You Don't

What the New Breed of CMOs Know That You Don't

MARYLEE SACHS

Routledge
Taylor & Francis Group

LONDON AND NEW YORK

First published 2013 by Gower Publishing

Published 2016 by Routledge
2 Park Square, Milton Park, Abingdon, Oxfordshire OX14 4RN
711 Third Avenue, New York, NY 10017, USA

First issued in paperback 2016

Routledge is an imprint of the Taylor & Francis Group, an informa business

British Library Cataloguing in Publication Data
A catalogue record for this book is available from the British Library.

The Library of Congress has catalogued the printed edition as follows:
Sachs, MaryLee.
  What the next generation of CMOs know that you don't / by MaryLee Sachs.
    pages cm
  Includes bibliographical references and index.
  ISBN 978-1-4094-5572-1 (hardback)
  ISBN 978-1-4724-0404-6 (epub) 1. Marketing executives. 2. Marketing--Management.
  I. Title.
  HF5415.13.S2325 2013
  658.8--dc23

                                                                                    2013003999

ISBN 13: 978-1-138-27188-3 (pbk)
ISBN 13: 978-1-4094-5572-1 (hbk)

Contents

List of Figures

List of Tables

List of Photographs

List of Abbreviations

ANA	Association of National Advertisers
AOPs	Annual Operating Plans
AOR	Agency-of-Record
AR	Analyst Relations
B2B	Business-to-Business
B2C	Business-to-Consumer
BoD	Board of Directors
BU	Business Unit
CCO	Chief Communications Officer
CEO	Chief Executive Officer
CFO	Chief Financial Officer
CIO	Chief Information Officer
CMO	Chief Marketing Officer
COO	Chief Operating Officer
CRM	Customer Relationship Management
CSR	Corporate Social Responsibility
CTO	Chief Technology Officer
CVP	Corporate Vice President
EFT	Electronic Funds Transfers
EVP	Executive Vice President
FMCG	Fast-moving Consumer Goods
GE	General Electric Company
GM	General Manager
HR	Human Resources
IBM	International Business Machines
IOT	Internet of Things
KPI	Key Performance Indicators
MMM	Market Mix Modeling
OEM	Original Equipment Manufacturer
P&G	Procter & Gamble
P&L	Profit-and-Loss
PR	Public Relations
R&D	Research and Development
ROI	Return on Investment
ROMI	Return on Marketing Investment
VP	Vice President

About the Author

MaryLee Sachs is an independent marketing consultant and launched her first book, *The Changing MO of the CMO — How the Convergence of Brand and Reputation Has Affected Marketers*, at the Cannes Lions International Festival of Creativity in 2011. In 2012, she established her consultancy, Changing MO LLC, based on the tenets of that book, and she advises CMOs on navigating change, discipline and channel integration, influencer strategies and international best practice. *What the New Breed of CMOs Know That You Don't* is MaryLee's second book.

Previously, MaryLee was the President and CEO/US and former worldwide Head of Consumer Marketing at a major WPP firm where she spent her most recent years focused on the CMO community. She has contributed to both The CMO Club and the Marketing 50 as an advising member, and she has been a member of the Marketing Group of Great Britain for over 15 years. She also recently joined the Global Marketing Network as an advisory council member and faculty member.

MaryLee has over 28 years of integrated marketing experience in the international arena, working with and advising many blue-chip brands including Procter & Gamble, American Express, Motorola, Kellogg's, PepsiCo, HSBC, Patek Philippe, Porsche, Anheuser-Busch, and many others. In many cases, strategic direction and campaign execution spanned the European region or were international in nature, and most assignments included integration across the marketing disciplines.

MaryLee was resident in London for 17 years before returning to the US 11 years ago. She lives in New York City with her husband and two dogs.

Email: marylee@changingmo.com
Web: www.changingmo.com
Twitter: @maryleesachs
LinkedIn: www.linkedin.com/pub/dir/Marylee/Sachs/

Acknowledgements

Researching my first book created an innate curiosity about the CMO role in its entirety, especially given the rapidly changing dynamics of the marketing ecosystem and the increased challenge for organizations to grow given macroeconomic trends. What started as a research project for my new consultancy translated into a need for me to document the experiences and views of some game-changing marketers.

I am eternally grateful to my network of friends and business contacts for helping me with my research, particularly those CMOs who agreed to be interviewed, who allowed me to peer into their organizations and, by doing so, contributed to and curated this book. All of them are to be congratulated for leading change in their organization, going boldly where no one has been before.

- Asim Zaheer, SVP, Worldwide Marketing, Hitachi Data Systems

- Carin Van Vuuren, CMO, Usablenet

- Carlos Zepeda, VP, Marketing, Alpargatas USA/Havaianas

- Christine Heckart, CMO, ServiceSource

- Danielle Tiedt, CMO, YouTube

- Douwe Bergsma, CMO, Georgia–Pacific

- Elisa Steele, CMO, Skype, and CVP, Marketing, Microsoft

- Erin Nelson, CMO, Bazaarvoice

- Ian Drew, EVP, Marketing and Business Development, ARM

- Jack Armstrong, Director, Marketing Communications North America, BASF

- Jeff Jones, EVP and CMO, Target Corporation

- Jonathan Becher, CMO, SAP

- Julie Woods-Moss, CMO, Tata Communications

- Marc de Grandpre, CMO, KIND Snacks

- Marcy Shinder, Head of Global Marketing, Nielsen

- Martine Reardon, CMO, Macy's

- Maryam Banikarim, SVP and CMO, Gannett Corporation

- Michael Sneed, VP, Global Corporate Affairs, Johnson & Johnson

- Michelle Peluso, Global Consumer Chief Marketing and Internet Officer, Citigroup

- Mike Ma, Head of Retail Advertising and Prospect Marketing, Vanguard

- Nigel Burton, CMO, Colgate-Palmolive

- Scott Ballantyne, Global CMO, Fab.com

- Scott Moffitt, EVP, Sales and Marketing, Nintendo North America

- SP Shukla, President, Group Strategy, and Chief Brand Officer, Mahindra Group

- Susan Lintonsmith, Global CMO, Quiznos

I would also like to thank business associates who provided stimulus and philosophical conversations as I ordered my thoughts including: Dave Allen of Brand Pie, Mhairi McEwan of Brand Learning, Caren Fleit of Korn/Ferry International, and Greg Welch and Tom Seclow of Spencer Stuart.

And I'm extremely grateful to some of my business associates for contributing further to my thinking and for making introductions to some of their CMO friends. Thank you to Andy McGowan, Ann Marshman, Bob Jeffrey, Caren Fleit, Christa Carone, Dave Allen, David Wilkie, Ellen Ryan-Mardiks, Hayes Roth, Jim Stengel, Jennifer Friedberg, Jenny Rooney, John Gerzema, Jonah Bloom, Kate Bullis, Kate Purcell, Lori Senecal, Maddie Hamill, Pat Verduin, Paul Taaffe, Pete Krainik, Rob Malcolm, Rosemarie Ryan, Scott Goodson, Shona Seifert, and Tony Burgess-Webb.

A special thanks goes to Tony Burgess-Webb, not just for connecting me to relevant sources, but for his introduction to my publisher, Jonathan Norman at Gower Publishing, who in turn prompted me to write a second book. Thank you both for your encouragement.

Finally, I'd like to thank my husband, Malcolm Beadling, for giving over "his" home office to me in aid of the cause. And my two office companions who kept me company—Stanley, our border terrier, and Harry, our miniature schnauzer.

Introduction

This book should be viewed as a "primer" for any new or aspiring chief marketing officer (CMO), C-suite peer to marketing, or marketer looking to "up their game," and as such it provides a range of ideas, concepts, approaches, and considerations from a wide range of CMOs who are driving significant transformation within their organizations.

The CMO is arguably the least understood executive in the C-suite by both the outside world and internal audiences. Job specifications differ widely—much more than for the chief executive officer (CEO), chief financial officer (CFO), or chief talent officer.

In some organizations, marketing can be seen as somewhat of a "black box" confused with sales, and which is sometimes viewed as a financial drain on the organization, funding expensive advertising campaigns, sponsorships and other untold extravagant line items. And while marketing may be the least understood business function, "everyone thinks they are a good marketer," as one interviewee for the book remarked on a panel of senior marketers at the Cannes Lions International Festival of Creativity in 2012.

In the best case scenario however, marketing is seen as a "must have" generator of business growth, innovation and reputation. As organizations look to differentiate and expand, marketing has taken on new prominence across the enterprise and at the boardroom table. "Highly effective CMOs are moving well beyond the longstanding role of being the proxy for the customer to one in which they provide strategic leadership, drive change, and achieve quantifiable business results," according to Caren Fleit, senior client partner of executive search firm Korn/Ferry International.[1] "In short, today's CMOs are more intertwined with the business and are expected to contribute to fundamental business transformation."

---

1   Fleit, C. 2012. *The Evolution of the CMO*. CNBC guest blog. [Online, May 15, 2012]. Available at: http://www.cnbc.com/id/47389582/Fleit_The_Evolution_of_the_CMO [accessed: November 24, 2012].

A practical example of how organizations are up-leveling marketing is within Kimberly–Clark as reported in *Advertising Age*.[2] "The process started with a decision five years ago to create a marketing and innovation committee on the board ... which would guide growth for the company in the same way you have an audit committee or a compensation committee. It was, for us, a completely new idea, and I don't actually know many companies that do that," according to Tony Palmer, the company's SVP and CMO at the time but who was promoted to president of global brands and innovation in 2012.

In the research for this book, 26 CMOs were interviewed from a range of business-to-consumer (B2C), business-to-business (B2B) and both B2C and B2B organizations. In all cases, their roles were different to what had gone before. That is to say, they had been appointed within the last two years to a newly-created role, a heightened role, or a role requiring significant restructuring or rethinking. These marketers come from start-ups, emerging players and turn-around situations, to large corporates looking to elevate the power of marketing in their organizations.

Business to Consumer	Both B2C and B2B	Business to Business
Citi	BASF	Arm
Colgate-Palmolive	Gannett	Bazaarvoice
Fab.com	Mahindra	Hitachi Data Systems
Georgia-Pacific	Skype	Nielsen
Havaianas	Target	SAP
Johnson & Johnson	Travelers	ServiceSource
KIND Snacks	Vanguard	Tata Communications
Macy's	YouTube	Usablenet
Nintendo		
Quiznos		

Figure I.1   CMOs Table

While there are many differences in the job descriptions, the marketers taking on these new CMO roles have some remarkable characteristics in common. According to an article published by *Marketing Management* in the Spring of 2012: "The chief information officer, chief technology officer or CMO who thrives as a member of the senior leadership team will be a team player who can lead without rank and has built an organization that earns the respect of the rest of the business. The skills that are increasingly in favor

---

2   Neff, J. 2011. How Kimberly-Clark is Lifting Sales by Elevating Marketing. *Advertising Age*. [Online, November 7, 2011]. Available at: http://adage.com/article/news/kimberly-clark-lifting-sales-elevating-marketing/230832/ [accessed November 28, 2012].

are strong communication, willingness to partner and strategic thinking ... For CMOs to thrive and survive in a collaborative C-suite, they will have to adopt a general management mindset and earn the respect of the others with fact-based analyses. They will be accountable for the brand strategy, driving the organic growth agenda and positioning the business for the future. As the acknowledged voice of the customer and consumer, they will ensure the strategy is built and executed from the outside in. They can no longer be passive service providers, content to oversee market insight activities, coordinate relationships with key marketing partners and ensure compliance 'reasonably' with brand guidelines."[3]

One of the co-authors of this article was Rob Malcolm, former president of global marketing, sales and innovation at Diageo and current lecturer at Wharton Business School. Malcolm spoke at a Conference Board CMO master class[4] in November 2012 and stressed the dual leadership challenge for CMOs to demonstrate, first and foremost, business leadership, and then marketing leadership.

Dual challenges

Business Leadership	Marketing Leadership
Earn the right to lead – adopting a general manager mindset	Be the voice of the customer
Establish a performance culture	Advocate for the brand
Have a vision for the future	Demonstrate performance – ROMI
Support (& alignment with) the CEO	Be the external radar
Develop business strategy	Ensure appropriate marketing capability + continuous learning & upgrading is in place
Innovate	Innovate
Flex with the role – driver, facilitator, collaborator	Leverage new technology
Develop key peer partnerships (CFO, COO, HR, CTO/CIO)	Retain & acquire appropriate talent
	Engender disciplined & creative culture

Figure I.2   Dual Challenges

3   Day, G.S., Malcolm, R. 2012. The CMO and the Future of Marketing. *Marketing Management Magazine*. Spring 2012 Edition, 34–43.
4   November 8, 2012 Conference. *New/Next CMO: A Master Class for Current and Aspiring CMOs*. The Conference Board. [Online]. Available at: https://www.conference-board.org/conferences/conferencedetail.cfm?conferenceid=2414 [accessed: November 11, 2012].

"The successful CMO embraces the dual business leadership and marketing leadership roles. He or she must work harder at the general business leadership role as they do at the role of leading the marketing because these are the newer challenges that they are less well prepared for ... Too often CMOs focus on the marketing role only and this is to their peril. They need to establish their executive/business/leadership credentials as priority number one, and have a concrete strategy to do so," he said.

All of the CMOs interviewed for the book demonstrated these characteristics. Several brought experience in operational roles to their marketing positions, bringing a new level of business acumen and fluency to the practice of marketing in their organizations.

Other common strengths included the strong desire to collaborate across the enterprise, a fearlessness to experiment and learn from both success and failure, a dedication to soliciting creativity and innovation from all employees — not just those in the marketing department, and a passion for recruiting, developing and retaining the best talent.

Interestingly, these CMOs are remarkably aligned on the importance of culture in the organization, and the role they can play in helping to shape a positive and productive mindset.

But the CMO role is increasingly not for the faint of heart. According to Fleit: "What we hear consistently from CMOs is that the world is changing, what they're facing is changing, and as a result, their role is changing. Nothing is the same as it was a couple of years ago." And as much as it has changed today, it will continue to change tomorrow.

1

The Changing Modus Operandi of the CMO

Job descriptions for a CMO role vary extremely widely. There are the traditional delineations—B2C and B2B roles, for example, can be very different. Industry sector and size of business also impact on the type of CMO role an organization adopts. Company history and culture, the CEO's mindset and C-suite support also factor into the make-up of a CMO. Personalities and interests of the CMO, as well, impact how the CMO approaches the task at hand.

Maryam Banikarim, SVP and CMO of Gannett Corp, Inc., talks about the CMOs who are members of the Marketing 50, a private community for senior-most marketers from globally respected organizations: "All those CMOs have very, very different jobs from each other. No two CMO jobs are alike. And it's increasingly a title that people just give out. It can just mean so many different things. And it's a different job at different companies."

According to Rob Malcolm, the CMO is "both the best of jobs and the worst of jobs at the same time."

Ultimately, the senior-most marketer of an organization is responsible for facilitating growth, sales and marketing strategy. He or she must work toward objectives such as revenue generation, cost reduction and/or risk mitigation. CMOs are faced with a diverse and growing range of disciplines in which they are required to be knowledgeable. And beyond the challenges of leading their own team, the CMO is invariably reliant upon resources beyond their direct control. Consequently, more than any other senior executive, the CMO must influence peers in order to achieve their own goals. Clearly this necessity to lead peers compounds the complexity of challenges faced by the CMO.

The somewhat unpredictable impact of marketing efforts coupled with the need to drive profits often leads to a short tenure for many CMOs. Global executive search firm Spencer Stuart researches and publishes an annual report on CMO tenure.[1] The good news is that the most recent study shows an all-time high of 43 months average, or roughly 3.5 years. However that's woefully lower than the average tenure of a CEO or even a CFO.

Table 1.1   CMO Tenure

Year	2004	2005	2006	2007	2008	2009	2010	2011
Months in Role	23.6	23.5	23.2	26.8	28.4	34.7	42	43

So what's behind the increase? According to Tom Seclow, who leads the North American Marketing Officer Practice for Spencer Stuart, the CMO is enjoying somewhat of an evolution. "CMOs are getting a lot of things right and gaining credibility among other C-suite members including CEOs. They've always been in the position of being the advocate for the customer in the organization. Now, largely because of the Internet and their [CMOs'] ability to leverage data and information, they can bring that into the organization in a quantifiable and meaningful way. Their ability to quantifiably describe not just who, but why and how customers are buying products and services is core to the business."

According to Seclow, there's a new breed of CMOs. They have the technical qualities of course, but the CMO mandate now is so much broader. While they must have some technical understanding of all of the areas of marketing, they have specialists underneath them to execute programs, so the CMOs themselves have to be really good at leading the team and providing strategic direction, and they need to build credibility from their C-suite peers, particularly their CEO. In the past, it used to be that the CMO was the keeper of the brand and the creative guru—much more intuitive and not necessarily the type of person to be put in front of an industry analyst or financial analyst. Things have changed.

"And one of the phenomenons that we have seen," Seclow continued, "is that there are more and more companies that look for marketing needs outside their industry. A common lament we hear is 'Hey, we know our industry sector really well, but we don't know the marketing function as well.' So 40 percent of our top marketing officer placements last year were working in a different

---

1   *Chief Marketing Officer Tenure Now at 43 Months.* [Online, July 5, 2012]. Available at: http://www.spencerstuart.com/about/media/72 [accessed: November 20, 2012].

industry than the one we put them in." He reasons that marketing is a more transportable skill set—to be able to connect with customers or consumers regardless of industry—that is the skill of identifying and communicating and relating to your customer is what's core to a CMO's success.

Balance is important too. According to by Lisa Arthur, CMO of Aprimo and contributor to the Forbes CMO Network, "Today's CMOs are more accountable than they have been in the past. Marketing has always been part art. But, these days, it's part science, too. Data-driven talent and big data analytics give CMOs the insights they need to truly propel the business forward. Many CMOs are also leveraging technology to automate much of the work, and as a result, they have become more focused on driving top line growth … and once that special sauce is found between a CMO and a chief information officer (CIO)/CFO, no CEO or BoD [board of directors] wants to start tinkering." Put simply, "the answer is simple. CMO tenure is on the rise because CMOs are hitting their stride as change agents."[2] Of course there's an exception to every rule, and one CMO interviewed recently joined his organization where he was the third CMO in 50 years. Jeff Jones joined Target in 2012, following the two previous CMOs who spent over 20 years each with the retailer. He is also the first person that was hired from the outside and put straight onto the executive group.

At its very core, the CMO is supposed to have responsibility for the "4 Ps of marketing"—promotion, pricing, products and services, and placement (distribution). In 2012, IBM built on its 2011 global CMO study "From Stretched to Strengthened,"[3] which surveyed over 1,700 CMOs in 64 countries, with a State of Marketing Survey 2012.[4] In that survey, IBM reported that "many high-performing organizations already recognize the fact that marketing can, and should, take a more active role in leading the customer experience."

In an October 2012 webcast entitled "Why Leading Marketers Outperform" hosted by the IBM Center for Applied Insights, IBM built on its CMO insights with a survey of marketing professionals from around the world across more than 15 industries, cross-referencing financial performance. The results further

---

2   Arthur, L. June 2012. *CMOs Are Now Sticky…Here's Why*. Blog, Forbes CMO Network. [Online, June 21, 2012]. Available at: http://www.forbes.com/sites/lisaarthur/2012/06/21/cmos-are-now-sticky-heres-why [accessed: November 20, 2012].

3   *From Stretched to Strengthened—Insights from the IBM Global CMO Study*. Released October 14, 2011 [Online]. Available at: http://www-935.ibm.com/services/us/cmo/cmostudy2011/cmo-registration.html [accessed: November 11, 2012].

4   IBM Press Release. 2012. *IBM Survey Reveals Marketers Face Tech Dilemma in Reaching the Connected Consumer*. [Online, June 21, 2012]. Available at: http://www-03.ibm.com/press/us/en/pressrelease/38084.wss [accessed: November 27, 2012].

strengthened the importance of owning the "4 Ps": "leading marketers report greater effectiveness across all four of the classic marketing "Ps" ... They are more likely to assume an all-encompassing role, 'owning' the customer experience across channels and/or business functions. These marketing organizations also make spending decisions differently, employing a more analytical and cooperative approach. Often, line-of-business peers are part of the process, providing valuable input on the marketing mix."

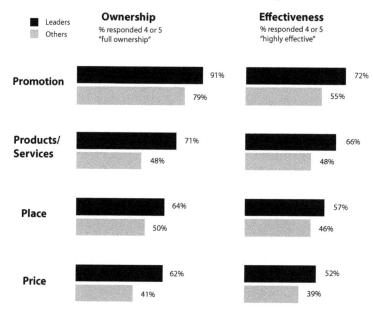

Figure 1.1   Influence of Marketing Organizations

But just as the marketing function continues to change and morph, Stephen Liguori, executive director of global innovation and new models at General Electric, suggests that there are three new "Ps" that marketers need to address—principles, people and process—which altogether serve to deliver better business results.

Interestingly, Elisa Steele, CMO of Skype (see page 26) also refers to "3 Ps" but these are defined as:

1. "our programs—where they are, what we want them to be and how do we deliver them;

2. our process—how do we be more efficient and not repeat the types of tasks that can either be done in automation or in a pooled

resource environment where everybody doesn't have to keep figuring things out on their own; and

3. people—making an investment in our people, not only bringing in talent where we have critical gaps of talent but also taking a really more thoughtful approach around career development for the people in the team and who have passion and the desire to excel here."

However it's viewed, marketing is expanding its role in organizations and touching business aspects not traditionally included in the marketing suite such as customer service, technology platforms, internal communications and, the pièce de résistance, setting enterprise-wide strategy.

Clearly, the CMO role is becoming increasingly complex given these added responsibilities, but CMOs are well-placed to deliver given their central role in the organization, the fact that they integrate across so many disciplines, their access to analytics, and their understanding of the customer and/or consumer.

In its white paper "The Transformative CMO,"[5] The Korn/Ferry Institute advocates that "the mandate for today's CMO is nothing less than fundamental business transformation." In this paper, Lauri Kien Kotcher, CMO of Godiva, is quoted: "Marketing is increasingly intertwined with all other functions in the company. CMOs need strong leadership skills to influence across the organization, cross-functionally, and geographically. We need to be able to adapt our plans based on rapid-fire feedback; this means moving together as an organization to drive results."

Senior marketers have always leveraged their creative and analytic abilities, but the growing complexity of the business environment, the leap in customer centricity and consumer power, and the rapid pace of change is creating the need for a new breed of "super-hero" CMO.

In its Deloitte Review paper entitled "From Mad Man to Superwoman,"[6] the authors say that, "If you ask industry observers to comment on the expectations

5   Fleit, C., Morel-Curran, B. 2012. *The Transformative CMO: Three must-have competencies to meet the growing demands placed on marketing leaders*. Korn/Ferry Institute Report. [Online, March 2012]. Available at: http://kornferryinstitute.com/reports-insights/transformative-cmo-three-must-have-competencies-meet-growing-demands-placed [accessed: November 27, 2012].
6   Gandhi, S., Rodriguez, G., Banks, G. 2012. *From Mad Man to Superwoman*. Deloitte Review, Issue 11. [Online, 2012]. Available at: http://www.deloitte.com/view/en_US/us/Insights/

versus the performance of CMOs today, there is a big delta. First, there is the notion of the 'super CMO,' which *Ad Age* has described as someone whose mission 'isn't just marketing, but strategy and overall growth' of the company, or the CMO as a 'super species' defined by *Media Post* as someone who has 'responsibility for functions including operations, finance and public policy.' Slightly less aggressive, but still elevated, is the idea—from one of the top talent recruiting firms—of the CMO as 'marketing's CEO'." Whatever the evolution of marketing is called, it's clearly being elevated as a management function, and organizations are expecting more and more of their senior marketers.

Browse-by-Content-Type/deloitte-review/31fd9ffe54088310VgnVCM3000001c56f00aRCRD. htm [accessed: November 27, 2012].

2

The Chosen Ones

As a CMO or an aspiring CMO, how does one get the gig of a lifetime?—that role that is life-changing, career-progressing and/or passion-fulfilling?

While not exactly statistically valid, the marketers who were interviewed for this book split roughly 50 percent appointed from outside the organizations, and the other 50 percent represented a combination of being promoted from within or from consulting the organization or they were connected personally. It's fair to say that as an organization looks to heighten the importance of marketing, the concept of appointing a "known quantity" to the senior-most role may be more appealing to some CEOs and boards. That said, there is the notion that "fresh blood" also is enticing when looking to adopt and promote significant change.

Onboarding

Once recruited or promoted, the onboarding experience for these marketers varied widely. Of course onboarding was more important to those who were recruited from outside the organization, however in many cases, even these CMOs were expected to hit the ground running, and many invested time before their first day on the job in an attempt to get up to speed in advance.

Onboarding ranged from extensive and quite formal programs designed to introduce the new CMO to key personnel and the business, to virtually being thrown into the deep end with a barrage of urgent matters—particularly true where the CMO position was a newly-created role. Generally speaking across all of the CMOs interviewed for the book, having a "first 90 days" period was a luxury for most. Those who did their homework before their first day on the job seemed to benefit from that investment in time, getting to know their teams, peers and board members in advance. "Listening" was a key element to learning as much about the business as possible.

For some CMOs, the onboarding was a do-it-yourself process. Susan Lintonsmith of Quiznos started her onboarding process prior to her first day. "I had an extensive interview process, meeting with each of the board members and key members of the private equity firm. I was actually on board committee calls and talked with franchise council members prior to even coming into the office for day one. So my onboarding process was really what I put in place, different from what I've done when I've hired people where I've actually set up introductory meetings with key people throughout the company for them and given them pre-reading information. I just stepped in and built my own onboarding process. But it started before I started."

Similarly, Target's Jeff Jones' arrival began before he arrived as well. Following a very extensive interview process, he spent a lot of time getting to know the business before day one. And he relates to his first day on the job, "When I was first introduced, literally in the first hour of day one in front of the entire marketing team, I spoke about my leadership expectations and the five words that shape me as a person and how I make decisions … Then I sent a love letter to the marketing leadership basically reiterating those things, and also 10 expectations for how I like to lead and do business. One of the big things I've tried to win on early here is setting a tone for communicating that's been very different from the past: open, frequent, transparent."

The five words? Listen, provoke, love, simplify and believe. Jones continued, "I also wanted to move faster than 90 days because we're a retailer and we live in a nimble world. So in my first 60 days, I've been able to establish a tone for communication. I've been able to paint a clear picture of the role of marketing at Target, and I've been able to do a first phase of [marketing team] realignment (see page 93)."

Carin Van Vuurin, the newly-appointed CMO of Usablenet—who had previously been a consultant to her company—said, "My onboarding experience was atypical, but not because I had familiarity with the organization. I think my onboarding was atypical because they [Usablenet executives] had never seen an animal like me before, and what I wanted to do in this onboarding is look under the hood of the organization, so we structured an onboarding program that was as much about understanding the business at the highest level as it was about getting into the nuts and bolts of the platform and the technology; in other words, everything that determines the sustainability of the business."

Erin Nelson of Bazaarvoice recalls, "So I was relatively familiar with what the company did, but the onboarding process was really, really fast. So it was basically like, 'hey Erin, show up and start making a difference tomorrow,' which I don't think is different than many CMOs, right? I think that there's such an urgency to drive growth and brand equity, I don't know anybody that gets any kind of grace period in their jobs. The same thing happened at Dell [her previous employer]. I was literally job negative 30 days in and already saddled with so many challenges. So it was a pretty aggressive ramp-up. The first week I was here I was already out with customers. I was already out with analysts. I was in Europe the second week I was here. So there no time for 'hey, welcome, here's how we do stuff, get started when you can'."

Nelson also recalls the one unique thing that Bazaarvoice does for everybody in their first week with the company—a scavenger hunt. "This company happens to be one that's been built on the idea that culture really drives great performance … So the one thing that everybody does, me included, is a scavenger hunt, which is 70–75 questions that really force you to navigate the company and talk to people that you otherwise wouldn't and learn things that you otherwise wouldn't. So the minute the scavenger hunt was over, that's when I hit the pavement."

At the other end of the spectrum, some onboarding processes were quite comprehensive. For Douwe Bergsma of Georgia–Pacific, "There are actually three levels of onboarding. One was the onboarding you would expect from a compliance and legal perspective. And I think that is an extremely well-structured, well-prepared, well-organized 30/60/90-day plan with reminders every week on what you still have to do, online courses, class courses, a meeting with the appropriate human resources (HR), legal and compliance managers. I think that was top onboarding, all nailed down from soup to nuts."

Bergsma detailed the other two levels of onboarding as the company's "market-based management onboarding," which is the management philosophy of Koch Industries, owner of Georgia–Pacific. This level of onboarding is based on the book, *The Science of Success*[1] by Charles G. Koch, and also included online and class courses, and mentorship. The third area was on-the-job onboarding:

---

1   Koch, C.G. 2007—1st Edition. *The Science of Success*. [Online, n.d.]. http://www.kochind.com/MBM/science_of_success.aspx [accessed: November 24, 2012].

"This was what we would call spontaneous order, and it's basically what you'd expect since there was no predecessor."

When Scott Moffitt joined Nintendo as its head of marketing for the Americas, he discovered a very comprehensive onboarding process. "It's a culture that's somewhat unique and different. And they had not done a great job of bringing people onboard. And learning from that, they had a very structured and very organized process—one of the most formal onboarding processes I've been involved with," he said.

"I spent a lot of time in one-on-one meetings with cross-functional peers, going deep in organizations. Really each week, I had meetings with multiple levels of people within one function or one part of the organization that I was going to be interacting with. And that was over maybe a six-week period. Meanwhile, I was busy doing the job but also I felt like I was studying each part of the organization or getting an indoctrination into each part of the organization. So one week, there would be two or three days of meetings with various people on the legal team. Another week, the operations team. Another week, another part of the organization. And so it really helped create a gradual on-ramp, although it did create a challenge because there was the demand to begin trying to put some points up on the board for what my responsibilities were going to be and to make sure I was interacting with my team. But also, there was this sort of added work or bonus work. But it did, I think, allow me to forge ties and bonds with the organization more quickly. And since we have a distributed office structure in the US, I have team members in three locations: San Francisco, New York, and Redmond, Washington. So that created a little bit of extra challenge."

Marcy Shinder of Nielsen came into her office the week before she started to get her name badge, security card and computer. "I just made sure that when I came in on day one, I was not wasting meaningful time getting set up." Shinder also wanted to adopt the right mindset. "Entering a new company requires a new mindset, and I wanted to start fresh in the new role. One helpful aspect was I literally put aside my entire wardrobe and went out and bought new clothes. The clothes were just a manifestation of the mindset and corporate culture." And like others, she also went on a listening tour: "I had two questions for our key business leaders around the world—1) what are your biggest opportunities and challenges? And 2) what do you want me to accomplish? And within 30 days, that basically informed my playbook."

90 days or not, Danielle Tiedt of YouTube posed a reality check in her interview. "When you read all those 90-day books, you get real panicked that by the end of 90 days, you should have your full plan. And I think that impression is not reality. I would say that it's more like 75 percent reality. I think a lot of people expect you to hit the ground running. But I do think that there's way more room to take some time to figure stuff out and for that to be valued."

Surprises

Whether onboarding was proactively planned or do-it-yourself, no level of familiarity could have prepared some of the CMOs interviewed for the surprises or challenges they encountered. But because these CMOs were accustomed to managing change, they managed to excel in the face of adversity—or at least dramatic shifts.

Susan Lintonsmith was called by the chairman of the board in the middle of her second week at Quiznos and was told that the board was replacing the CEO who had just hired her. "So at the beginning of week three, I had a new CEO in place. So when you talk about building relationships, for me I had spent time building a relationship and I was hired by one CEO, and then not even three weeks later I had a new CEO." But they were both new so Lintonsmith admits that the bonding was established quickly.

Carin Van Vuurin didn't expect that Usablenet would be launching a whole new evolution of the business at her 65-day mark. "But again, I guess I shouldn't have been surprised … It's a very competitive world, and I think that everyone is running very fast."

Some of the surprises came in the form of an internal mind-shift. Erin Nelson of Bazaarvoice experienced a bit of a shock that was based on transitioning from big powerhouse brands to a brand that wasn't top-of-mind for everyone. "When you tell people that you work at Dell or Procter & Gamble, it's like 'check,' I got that. When you say you work at Bazaarvoice, it's 'what?' And so there's just a lot that I do every day to evangelize the business we're in, and why we drive results. So I have a whole new talk track that I've never had to have for the first 20 years of my career."

3

The First CMO

CMOs exist in 62 percent of Fortune 500 companies[1] so it's not surprising to see fairly established organizations without CMOs decide that it's time to hire or promote one into the C-suite as differentiation and strategic marketing become more important to remain competitive.

The three organizations interviewed for this chapter include Tata Communications, Skype and Usablenet—two B2B players and one, Skype, which is both B2B (enterprise) and B2C.

Tata Communications

JULIE WOODS-MOSS, CMO, TATA COMMUNICATIONS

Julie Woods-Moss is the chief marketing officer of Tata Communications. She joined in December 2011 after consulting with the organization for over a year. She was previously at BT, and has held positions at United Pan-European Cable, part of Liberty Global, and IBM.

Julie Woods-Moss started working with Tata Communications on an interim basis, with the organization's Formula One sponsorship being the entrée. But given the size of that specific challenge, and

---

1   Seclow, T., Routhier, R., Brown, A., 2011. *Succeeding as an Organization's First Chief Marketing Officer.* [Online, June 2011]. Available at: http://www.spencerstuart.com/research/1505 [accessed: November 18, 2012].

other opportunities, she joined the company full-time officially in December 2011.

Tata Communications is a global telecommunications company based in Mumbai, and it has a submarine cable network of more than 235,000 kilometers.

According to Woods-Moss, "My first year with Tata was really trying to build a strategic relationship between these two firms [Tata Communications and Formula One] and that went brilliantly, and it's been an extremely successful period for both companies."

Woods-Moss emphasizes that the CEO, Vinod Kumar, sees marketing as very strategic and soon realized the complementary skills she brought to his executive team. This was quickly demonstrated by the initiatives that he engaged Woods-Moss in early on which had nothing to do with brand or marcomms, but more about the business and the customer experience.

Tata Communications is in the enviable position of being a $3 billion start-up at eight years old, growing at 30 percent per annum. When Tata was bought out of an Indian Government entity, Kumar was part of that 10-person team who bought the asset. "And he's actually grown the firm from half a dozen people to 7,000," according to Woods-Moss. Tata, the original parent company, remains a majority shareholder, and the Government remains a minority shareholder.

Woods-Moss joined an executive team which is widely disbursed geographically with members in Singapore, Delhi, Montreal, Washington DC and London, where she is based together with the head of enterprise sales. But Tata executives are brought together frequently. "Vinod is really a people person. He invests heavily in three forums. There's the global management committee which is the top board, but then he says everyone on that board really has two or three people who, without them, they can't get anything done, so he then created a G30—the global top 30 executives in the company, and it's an extraordinary commitment and resource, but they meet three or four times a year, with each meeting lasting two and a half days," Woods-Moss said. "And then the third group is a leadership forum group which is the top 250 people in the organization. Vinod speaks to this group every six weeks, and they meet twice a year," she continued.

The internal closeness within the management ranks runs through the entire workforce. Woods-Moss waxes lyrical about Tata Communications' use of Chatter, an enterprise-wide social media network and real-time collaboration platform for users, and an interesting crowd-sourcing cross-platform tool which was just launched. "It's called Tata Innoverse—Inno for innovate, and Verse for universe, like the universe for innovation. You can literally throw out a challenge and crowd-source ideas." It's even more significant given that the scope of the platform is not just for Tata Communications, but rather the whole of the Tata group which represents a workforce of one-half billion individuals.

Given that Woods-Moss's start with Tata Communications was on an interim basis, she talks about a fast ramp-up: "When you're an interim, you are a gun for hire. You're not expected to have any simulation period … I'm pretty much a tech person so that was a huge benefit. I started off as an encrypter so when you can really understand the offer, because it's a really complicated offer, the induction period is a little bit easier. And I was very fortunate that within a few weeks of being an interim, I was invited to the first top 30 meeting." She continues, "So I immediately met them all in San Francisco and the CEO was wonderful. He welcomed me and he said, 'Guys, your one mission in this meeting is to help persuade Julie to sign up permanently'."

"So that meeting was a tipping point for me actually because I wasn't looking for a new corporate role, but because it was run with such respect for the individuals and with no politics and no agenda, it was a big motivator for me. I could see that I would really enjoy being part of this because when you've had more freedom to operate, to choose who your clients are, I mean within reason, you can be very selective about the environments you think are healthy that you want to thrive in."

Culturally, Woods-Moss says that while Tata Communications is very international, "there's a very strong Indian heritage," and there are significant differences between an Anglo Saxon culture and Indian culture and Asian culture. She says, "We tend to earn the respect of each other. With the Asian and Indian culture, respect is automatically given to your superior. So actually getting open communication requires quite a significant investment in time in building trust."

According to Woods-Moss, the relationship between Kumar and his executive team represents genuine affection. "They challenge each other and it's very impressionable. It's based on a deep respect and affection for each other."

In terms of Woods-Moss's first 90 days, her first goal was to establish a center of excellence which included a number of shared services. So there was an organizational element. "My most important job was to get to know the people." She agreed with the CEO that it was important to establish a level of trust in terms of building a high-performing team, and she also walked into the last week of a six-month evaluation to select a new agency, so she concluded that process.

Woods-Moss is a firm believer in the axiom "If it's not broken, don't fix it," and although she didn't know if the choice of agency was the right one, she is pragmatic enough to focus on the organization's vision, and getting on with business. "I didn't need, as a new CMO, to have the glory of this new 'brush'," she says.

Sticking with the vision is key for Woods-Moss. "Our vision is around our purpose in a new world of communications which actually is quite a big space for us to be in, and there's a lot more we can do with that so actually, we have very clear corporate imperatives. So in terms of the brand, I think we're at an interesting stage in our development that the dizzy days of 50 percent growth, of acquire—acquire—acquire, creates an energy that permits 24/7 working, a slightly chaotic approach, no process, etc. Now we're at 30 percent growth in a sector that's growing in tiny percentages. It's a challenging world environment. People are getting a little fatigued. So now the brand really needs to start working to lift people, to give them a sense of purpose. We're focusing a lot on how we get more internal engagement with our purpose."

Her second goal or challenge was "just getting better cohesion and better impact in terms of the stories we tell," which followed the vision.

"The third priority is that this particular company is technology-led, engineering-led. They've never had a CMO. There was a very small product marketing team which was somewhat isolated from the business so a big priority of mine was to start to get some traction to set the marketing on a journey to becoming the headlights of the business."

Woods-Moss continues, "And for the transformation to be successful in this particular environment, it's about that—having a really tight coupling with product and that is time-consuming, it's challenging but not because of a lack of cooperation. It's challenging because our stuff's complex and actually to get it communicated in a way that a business leader, a CIO, would understand."

In terms of her team, because there wasn't a CMO before, the bulk of marketing talent reported to sales, the sectors and corporate communications. She inherited a 70-strong team with two direct reports, so, initially, she looked at pulling together the resources, identifying the gaps, and looking at how best to stretch and transform the team. Secondly, she looked at how best to beef up the top bench, "but not overly, and then to build a case to rebalance the marketing function so that it's proportionate to product management and the sales challenge." She continues, "My strategy is always that you earn the right with quick wins and then you go with a business case that says 'I could do more of this with additional resources'."

There has been no shortage of initiatives for Woods-Moss to achieve some quick wins. "The first thing was to get some proper workflow process so that we can now report on a monthly basis and with a high degree of confidence, as well as react to issues weekly … There wasn't any integrated marketing automation with the sales force. There was no customer database that has any value to marketing. So the first thing I agreed with the board is that we won't try to boil the ocean, but at least let's get the top 250 of our clients which account for 40 percent of the revenue properly in a database with some email automation."

Woods-Moss also reported a timely acquisition of a company expert in content distribution, and one of the company representatives took on a broader role which included marketing automation. So she moved all of the digital assets to him in order to progress marketing automation. And she's putting a lot of processes in place.

"The only thing I've just begun to realize is that I think fast and act fast and the team are now just exhausted. It's like 'Julie, we've got to get more resources.' We're getting to the point where it's 'enough already.' So this is now a big priority—to continue building the team."

Woods-Moss's remit is fairly all-inclusive which includes all communications—internal communications, corporate communications and analyst relations, brand, sponsorships, partner marketing, proposition and product marketing, geo and segment marketing, and all of the digital elements—Internet, intranet and social, advertising, competitive intelligence, insights, market planning and strategy. Investor relations sits in the corporate strategy group, with whom Woods-Moss works closely on annual and three-year planning.

As Woods-Moss gets her arms around the business, she faces some significant challenges. "The challenge is I have an embryonic network in India and it's such a big part of the business, so the amount of time initially that I should really spend in India versus my practical ability to do so is a constant challenge … The second challenge is that my default leadership style is a bit more instructive than what my team is accustomed to," she says. So on a personal level, she's needing to temper that while she's still in a hurry to get things done. "The third challenge is that the company has grown very fast but it's not a boardroom brand yet," she adds. This makes it challenging for the sales team to get into the doors of the big corporate players.

On the latter point, Woods-Moss is establishing a scorecard for the organization's center of excellence which will measure brand consideration, profitable growth and employee motivation. "We want to drive profitable growth; we want a world-leading portfolio; we want motivated employees who are our advocates in the market."

Woods-Moss has taken a novel approach to planning in an effort to bring together disparate groups. "Every team did their own thing so I said that in the first place, 'you're going to do your own plans, and then we're going to share them. I'm going to ask for 're-use,' so I'm going to ask each of you to drop 20 percent of your plan and steal from what someone else is planning.' So we did that in the first quarter, and I gave a special reward for the best contributor and the best re-user. And then I announced that in the second quarter we would work on some global programs together," she says. "I let them know that by the second half of the year, I wanted an integral plan because I've learned the hard way that if you come in new and take people's empowerment away and force centralized programs, they fail. So by demonstrating how they can work together, they get a benefit."

Key for Woods-Moss is elevating marketing in the organization. According to her, Kumar made that goal clear in that first meeting in San Francisco. "He said, 'Julie's transforming marketing. Marketing will be the headlights of the business—being strategic, understanding where we make our big bets'," she says.

Interestingly, Tata Communications operates an annual recognition program to celebrate failure. "You can win a lot of money and prestige if you have the best learning from a failure," according to Woods-Moss.

Usablenet

CARIN VAN VUURIN, CMO, USABLENET

Carin Van Vuurin assumed the position of CMO at Usablenet in June 2012. She has over 15 years' experience in brand-building and strategic marketing communications, most recently as executive director of corporate branding at WPP's Landor. Her industry experience includes working with brands such as Johnson & Johnson, UPS, KKR, JPMorgan Chase, Citigroup, Manpower and Pepsico.

Like Woods-Moss, Carin Van Vuurin consulted Usablenet while she was with branding firm Landor. "I tried to advise them in terms of how they should establish a foundation for their brand, think about brand building for the longer-term, and basically guide an organization that was 100 percent sales-oriented," she claims. As a technology company, she felt that the company's technology platform was well-developed, so the next step was to build a really successful sales organization built around brand. "I think that the organization had hit a plateau with its sales effort. I almost see the decision to start a really professional marketing organization as an inflection point in the growth of companies," she concluded.

Founded in 2000, Usablenet is a technology platform company that works with organizations to create a mobile web and multichannel presence. The company is headquartered in New York City, with offices in London, Milan and Los Angeles. It was named one of the top 10 most innovative companies in mobile commerce by Fast Company[2] in 2011, and can point to a number of blue-chip companies as clients including British Airways, JetBlue, Nissan, Dell, Expedia and Marks & Spencer.

While at Landor and over time, Van Vuurin started to act more as an advisor to the Usablenet team. CEO Nick Taylor ultimately reached out to her for advice on building a CMO role for the company, in her role as consultant. "So again, I continued my role as advisor. I think they went through quite a lot

---

2   The Top 10 in Mobile. *Fast Company*. [Online, March 2011]. Available at: http://www.fastcompany.com/most-innovative-companies/2011/top-10-mobile.php [accessed: November 4, 2012].

of iterations in terms of their own decision-making, and what kind of person they wanted in the role," she says.

Van Vuurin joined Usablenet as its CMO in June 2012. "I think it's an interesting balance between the very tactical with the absolute imperative to have somebody who can think big picture and conceptually where the business needs to go, and I increasingly realize that the challenges that an organization like Usablenet is facing is so aligned with my belief around how a brand should be built that when they approached me, and said, 'well, you know us, and we really think that this is something that is within your wheelhouse,' I started to take a much more serious look at it," she states.

Van Vuurin views her role as both "leader and builder:" "I'm building a fundamental infrastructure. I'm putting the bricks down for a sustainable organization. I'm managing the pieces that have been successful up until this moment, and I'm having to help people have a vision for what we can become over the long term." She continues, "I think organizations are needing to acquire a whole new skill set ... Not only do we need to acquire traditional marketing practices, we also need to learn current marketing practices, which is all about social media and social marketing, and the complexity of it—and I knew this going in. I'm now in an organization that de facto has shaped an entire industry, but how do you actually iterate on that thought leadership position?"

There are three people with whom Van Vuurin works most closely. She reports to the CEO, and she partners with the head of innovation and the global head of sales. And while she believes the CFO must be a significant stakeholder in the equation, within Usablenet, the CFO is more of a finance administrator because the CEO more directly controls the strategic financials of the organization, as it is independent and privately-funded.

Her marketing group is small—three people plus a five-person public relations (PR) agency team. She has one person leading PR, media and influencer liaisons; another directed to sales support, including campaign management and collateral; and a third is directed to client account management.

One aspect she finds missing is "brand." "In a traditional enterprise, you would find a brand person, whether that be creative services-oriented or brand management-oriented. There has not been that attention to the brand piece. Because I feel that brand is strategic marketing, I really do think that is an important piece. It also reflects my background, so I see that actually changing over time."

Given that Usablenet is a B2B business, Van Vuurin does not count advertising as one of her key responsibilities, but rather strategic PR, social media and general marketing as being the core pillars. Her PR agency is based on the West Coast of the USA, but she's also looking to add a new agency to the roster in the UK. "When you start thinking about the marketing, you need to start thinking about how does that expand, and it can't just be a US-centric strategy."

Van Vuurin already is working closely with sales. "I am a proponent that marketing and sales are two sides of one equation, so how can I not be partly responsible for enabling a sales goal to be achieved?" she reasons.

She has been quick to determine a path forward as well, and she sees the marketing strategy as being three-fold: "Setting direction for the company, influencing how we're building our business and our brand is first. Secondly, I definitely see marketing as a strategic influencer and the shaper of strategy … If I can achieve the kind of infrastructure and balance where marketing is fueling the sales engine, I would have achieved a tremendous amount, because right now I feel this organization is entirely push-oriented. When I can start to actually turn that around to where there is as much coming into the organization from pull as there is push, I would have materially influenced the success of this organization. Thirdly, I think that marketing can be seen as a partner as opposed to what I've seen in many organizations where marketing is basically the manufacturers of stuff, hosting of events and things like that."

In addition to a strategic approach to marketing, Van Vuurin is an advocate of internal marketing. "Partnering with our chief people officer in helping to shape what this culture should be, the behaviors that support our 'North Star,' and our purpose as an organization is crucial. It makes people feel like they know what's going on, and connected to the business," she says. "If you can't get the inside piece right, I don't think that you can be sustainable and successful over the long-term."

The internal communications piece also supports integration, particularly between marketing and sales. Van Vuurin sees her role as part enabler for the sales force: "You can create alignment by actually being very proactive in creating the tools that the sales force is going to use." And, like Tata

Communications, Usablenet uses Salesforce's Chatter. "It's a very good way to keep the updates going," she says.

The internal piece does not stop with current employees. Van Vuurin also has prospective employees in her sights: "I think this whole talent acquisition is imperative—when you're a relatively small organization and you want to build your bench with 'A' players, you have to work really hard to get 'A' players to notice you, despite the appeal and attractiveness of your brand. Negative comments carry twice the weight that they do if you were an established operation, so I think that employees, the internal audience, are disproportionately important when you are a small company."

Van Vuurin is circumspect about all that she needs to achieve, and she's infectious about her position: **"To be building a marketing organization and a successful brand in a fast changing environment … it's a little bit like trying to build something on a waterbed. It shifts at any point in time. But it's hugely exciting to be in our space."**

Skype

ELISA STEELE, CMO, SKYPE

Elisa Steele took on the newly-created role of CMO, Skype, and corporate vice president (CVP), marketing, Microsoft in July 2012. It is the third time Steele has taken on a newly-defined CMO post, most recently at Yahoo! where she spent three years as executive vice president (EVP) and CMO, and before at NetApp where she was senior vice president (SVP) of corporate marketing.

Unlike Woods-Moss and Van Vuurin, Elisa Steele didn't have any previous connections with Skype. Rather, a former colleague expressed interest in introducing her to some Microsoft executives, so she spent two days meeting with the leadership there, and that quickly translated into a discussion with Tony Bates, president of the Skype Division at Microsoft.

Bates was named Skype's CEO in 2010, where he oversaw the sale of the company to Microsoft for $8.5 billion about one year later (October 2011).

Although the time between the initial conversations with Microsoft and Steele's first day was fast—about 45 days—her onboarding process was comprehensive. "Microsoft has probably the best onboarding process I've ever seen for an executive coming into the company. It's very thoughtful and personalized with great intent to set you up for success ... it was a fantastic experience," says Steele.

Having said that, she was anxious to get started and came into the office early. "I actually couldn't wait to get started so I was in the office two weeks before I was even on the payroll and started talking with people. Because I just wanted to listen, just wanted to understand where they were at and what the experience had been." Steele talked with everybody, getting input from not just the marketers but also folks in engineering and operations, assessing what they wanted from marketing.

There was an added element of newness to the role, too, given that the Microsoft acquisition was relatively fresh, less than one year before Steele joined the organization in August 2012.

Steele is a three-time "new" CMO, that is, appointed to a newly-defined CMO position, first at NetApp, then at Yahoo!, and now at Skype. And she claims that, like most other appointments, she has taken a 100-day approach. **"I knew inherently that we needed to be really good story-tellers. And that if there is a company and a brand that can tell great stories, shouldn't it be Skype? So I immediately started working on a foundational capability of what makes up a good story, and how marketing can lead the way,"** she claims.

While Skype had had a marketing function previously, it was not integrated across the organization. "It was all over the place and therefore, it was nowhere. There is some great talent here and some great marketing work that's been done. And it's been done in small teams that are not connected. So by default, they could only have so much impact because they weren't working at a unified level ... Now, we're having all of the different functions contribute to fewer initiatives and do them better. It's the 'fewer bigger better' approach."

Steele continues, "Now we're going forward with the six key initiatives which are six go-to-market approaches of how to engage with our audiences and three fundamental capabilities that we want to build in the organization: story-telling, digital/social capability and user insights. And those are the three things I'm making investments in for team training, through outside resources, best practices, connections in the industry."

Steele's team is split between Skype's offices in Palo Alto, California, Microsoft's headquarters in Redmond, Washington, and London, England. She has moved to a functional structure, and de-duplicated roles between the three locations to alleviate confusion. And to support the camaraderie and local flavor, she has senior leaders in each location that she holds responsible for bringing the whole team together to talk about initiatives regardless of reporting lines.

"This is one restructure I've done—and I've done four restructures in my career that were very dramatic—where there has been more change appetite. I'm getting a lot of support, and that helps us all to be successful," she says.

"We went through this process to develop a unified mission in the midst of the restructuring of the team … And I'm discovering that people love Skype. Any great consumer brand aspires to brand love. That's the ultimate. And it was amazing to me to find not only how much brand love Skype has with its users but how much users use that word. Even when I got this job, I got 'Hi Elisa, I heard you're working at Skype. I love Skype. Let me tell you my story.' And it just happens," she claims.

This premise gave her the inspiration for working with the team to build a mission statement aiming to build the best relationship and collaboration between product and marketing. "It has to be memorable. It has to be inspiring, and it has to be long-lasting. And so, what we ultimately came up with is three words and not only the team rallied around those three words, but I have product managers asking me 'when are you getting the T-shirts?'" she states.

That mission is "Build user love." Steele explains, "The 'build' is around the hard work that we want to put in because building something is not easy and it's also a signal to the product organization that they build great products and we support you. The 'user' is about putting the user in everything that we know, into the center of decision-making and into our hearts of how we move forward with the brand. And then obviously the 'love' is what I just team up with everything else." She adds that someone in her team got so inspired that they created a visual formula.

Figure 3.1   Build User Love Graphic

Steele continues by saying that the big accomplishment is that the mission is deeply believed in, and now she and her team are building off that, operationalizing it with her team and peers.

She believes in collaboration—within a function as well as across a function. "And I also believe that an executive staff member has their function to run but they also have the company to support and to run as well." Taking a leaf from Rob Malcolm's "Dual Leadership Challenge" notion, Steele says, "I absolutely believe that you play two roles: one as an executive and one as the leader of your function. And frankly, as an executive sometimes the right thing to do is not to invest in your function because there's something more important going on in the company … So I came in not only to learn and listen from the organization that I'd be running but to know my peers … And because this role didn't have that connection in the past, it becomes even more important."

Steele reports directly to Bates, who in turn reports to Microsoft CEO Steve Ballmer, and sits on his executive committee together with her peers on product, finance, HR, legal and business development. Her responsibilities are best described across the nine functions she has reorganized to: 1) insights and user intelligence, 2) product marketing—consumer, and 3) product marketing—enterprise, 4) brand, 5) audience marketing, 6) planning, 7) marketing operations, 8) integrated communications, and 9) advertising which includes everything Skype does to communicate with media, analysts, internal employees, the blogosphere, social.

While Steele works toward both her short-term objectives as well as longer-term goal to "build user love," she's clearly passionate about the brand and its capabilities, and how they can be applied to new initiatives, such as the Skype in Classroom public program which invites teachers to collaborate on classroom projects to share skills and inspiration around specific teaching needs. So far, 40,000 teachers have signed up and use it to connect classrooms and share lessons around the globe. Steele is a huge champion.

Summary

Being the first CMO appointed in an organization with fully-integrated responsibilities across the function provides an enormous opportunity to create something from scratch, to start with a blank sheet of paper. But with that opportunity comes the responsibility for creating infrastructure, processes and metrics that will stand the measure of time—not just charting early wins but providing the ability to analyze success over a longer period. These CMOs are building on their experiences to create a sustainable marketing approach which is built on teamwork and collaboration, and a keen eye on business results working with their peers and colleagues in sales and operations.

4

The Start-Up CMO

While start-ups tend to be focused on the product and its delivery, oftentimes the idea of bringing on a CMO or nominal head of marketing may seem a bit too extravagant until some traction is built in the business. But once there is some momentum, founders and CEOs of start-up organizations tend to realize that they could benefit from having a marketing professional on board to build the appropriate capabilities, develop and execute a plan of action, and integrate strategically with the business aims.

KIND Snacks

MARC DE GRANDPRE, HEAD OF MARKETING, KIND SNACKS

Marc de Grandpre assumed the newly-created role of head of marketing at KIND in September 2012. Previously, he was CMO of IMAX, VP of consumer marketing at Firethorn, a Qualcomm company, and managing director of Red Bull (sports) and marketing director of Red Bull (beverages).

KIND was conceived in 2003 by its founder, social entrepreneur Daniel Lubetzky. In 2009, Lubetzky was recognized by *TIME Magazine* among "25 Responsibility Pioneers" and *BusinessWeek* named him among "America's Most Promising Social Entrepreneurs." According to its website,[1] "KIND is a brand of all natural whole nut and fruit bars made from ingredients you can see and pronounce and it's also a movement that gives new purpose to

1   *Our Story* [Online, n.d.]. Available at: http://www.kindsnacks.com/our-story [accessed: October 19, 2012].

snacking … KIND was founded on the principle of holistic kindness, and we pride ourselves on creating new paths that avoid false compromises. Instead of 'Or' we say 'And.' We choose healthy and tasty, convenient and wholesome, economically sustainable and socially impactful."

KIND had an early win in 2009 with its distribution efforts. "As part of Starbucks' initiative to offer more healthy food along with its mochachinos, lattes and scones, the coffee chain began selling Lubeztky's KIND bars."[2] Starbucks remains a much-valued distribution partner and KIND also now has wide distribution through the grocery sector, such as Whole Foods and regional chains, and beyond.

Marc de Grandpre got a call from Lubetzky in 2009 for a reference on a previous colleague, and thus, a relationship was kindled. So when he got the call about the newly-created CMO position in May 2012, he jumped. "I just like what KIND stands for as a brand," he said.

Interviewed for this book 13 days into his new role, de Grandpre already was covering a lot of ground. His onboarding process was fully immersive and "very well orchestrated," and he was getting up to speed much faster than he had expected.

With a team of 38 including seven direct reports, de Grandpre allows that it was a fairly large team for the size of the business, but many were in field marketing. "They're young, very young," he admits, "but very talented, smart individuals. They just need a little more guidance, structure and training on how to manage projects, agencies, and become more creative by pushing the boundaries of creativity. So if there are any changes, it would be additions."

His responsibilities are "everything marketing, so anything that has to do with digital media including social, traditional media, field marketing, grass roots events, partnerships, communications (PR), online sales, metrics and analytics. And I'm touching new product development managing indirectly but very involved."

While it was early days for de Grandpre's interview, he already had established some priorities. "We don't have enough data on our consumers,"

---

2   Perman, S. 2009. KIND Bars Land in Starbucks. *Business Week*. [Online, June 30, 2009]. Available at: http://www.businessweek.com/stories/2009-06-30/kind-bars-land-in-starbucks [accessed: October 19, 2012].

he said. "And, we have some basic benchmarks in terms of awareness and conversion, but I'm not sure it's right. So we're going to clean that up a bit. But we have no insight into who our core consumer is. It's more anecdotal. So we've got to define that as a first priority because I think it's the way we will look at our new product development and our marketing. We've got to be anchored somewhere," he adds.

Another area of need and opportunity on which de Grandpre is focused is social media. "We have no one person focused on that so that's number one, and I got a hire approved yesterday." He explained that the current modus operandi on social is splitting it up among team members, but he wants consistency of voice, tone and message.

Similarly, on the agency side, KIND has a lot of agencies touching the business, but no agency of record, no one on retainer. De Grandpre claims that, "I don't think we need an agency of record. We mainly need to just streamline our roster of who we work with as a brand. We lack consistency somehow."

At a peer level, de Grandpre views his counterparts in sales, finance and especially operations as critical partners. With operations, he said, "We've got to build our marketing activation plan over a number of years and we've got to enable Bob [head of operations] to properly manage our resources, our line management, our manufacturing planning."

De Grandpre sits on the executive committee which is a small, close-knit group consisting of Lubeztky, the president, and the head of operations. In 2008, Lubeztky sold a minority share in KIND to VMG Partners, a private equity firm that specializes in investing in and building branded consumer product companies in the lower middle market, and VMP representatives sit on the KIND board.

It's early days for de Grandpre, but he already understands what the big hurdles will be going forward. "Definitely aligning the team and the structure within marketing because they were operating separately in corporate marketing, field marketing, communications and online sales … They are the young generation, very dynamic and want to be promoted today. So I'm trying to instill in them patience, teamwork and cross-pollination." And he's going to be focusing on KIND's partners, consumers and customers initially.

Moving forward, there is plenty of scope for growth in the US, but KIND has set its sights on international expansion, too, with plans to enter the Canadian market within the next few months. KIND Snacks already are sold in Mexico through a broker's agreement, and its products can also be found in 15 additional markets outside the US.

Fab.com

SCOTT BALLANTYNE, GLOBAL CMO, FAB.COM

Scott Ballantyne assume the role as global CMO for Fab.com in March 2012. Previously, he was CMO of Vonage. He has held senior marketing roles for Hewlett-Packard, Dell, T-Mobile, Tendrill, Global Crossing and Motorola Semiconductors.

Scott Ballantyne came into his newly-created CMO role at Fab.com through an unusual connection. He personally knew the founder and CEO, Jason Goldberg, because Jason has worked for Scott in a previous incarnation as a member of his marketing team at T-Mobile in Seattle. "We stayed friends ever since. We both say that he's tried for 10 years to have me work for him, and I've tried for 10 years not to work for him. But this was a no-brainer," according to Ballantyne.

Ballantyne reflects back on his recruitment: "One of the things here is that we are incredibly transparent. Just go read Jason's blog. He blogs veraciously about what he thinks, what he sees, what he does, and he wears his heart on his sleeve. So I knew before I came what to expect. He actually teased me one day back in November [2011] … he posted a Facebook page and said he was looking for a CMO. 'Scientists only may apply.' But my undergrad degree is in astrophysics. Don't ask me why!"

Goldberg had first started with social networking site Fabulis, which morphed into Fab.com—the marketplace for everyday design—which was launched June 2011. Goldberg believes you hire people as you scale, and since he personally had a heavy hand in the marketing, Fab.com didn't get to the point of needing a CMO until 2012. Ballantyne joined in February to "run global marketing which includes everything from branding to advertising to business development to communications to social strategy to analytics and overall strategy." According to Ballantyne, "If you look at the old fashioned marketing paradigms, the four Ps—product, placement, promotion and pricing, I do not have product because the product itself, that is the physical website and the merchandizing, is a cross-company collaboration."

Fab.com has quickly scaled and by July 2012, the company had more than five million members in 20 countries across the Americas and Europe. Fab reached one million members in just five months—faster than Facebook, Groupon and Twitter, according to Ballantyne. The company has worked with over 5,000 design partners, and has a company headcount of around 500. His marketing team is 16 strong including five direct reports. He has one team member based in Europe. He reports directly to Goldberg and is a member of a small C-suite including Goldberg; Bradford Shellhammer, the co-founder and chief creative officer; Beth Ferreira, COO; David Lapter, CFO; and a new chief people officer. As Ballantyne says, "I was the last C officer to join."

In terms of challenges, Ballantyne immediately lays claim to needing more people. "I needed a really interesting balance, and I thought it would be easier. I think we found some really good analytical marketers, but they didn't fit the Fab culture. And what I learned here more than anywhere else is the culture of what we hire is more important than the resume and what they do. It's more about how they do it. So we're actually prepared to take a B+ athlete that was just amazingly Fab culture appropriate, and drive them to an A as opposed to finding As and finding them to be horribly non-cultural." He adds, "It's on our sleeves. We're transparent. We are quirky. We always put customers first. We're prepared to make mistakes. There's very little hierarchy."

Ballantyne was interviewed for this book nine months into the role. One of the first things he did was to bring scale to the customer acquisition machine in terms of increasing channels, looking at the return, and re-stimulating non-active members. Another challenge was to move Fab into more consumer-facing media as opposed to the tech press, and for the brand to go global. Much of the media play is via PR, and Ballantyne has a agency in the US and in Europe, based in Germany—as Fab's largest market in Europe, and he is looking now at how best to cross-pollinate ideas and activities.

Key performance indicators (KPIs) for Ballantyne across the marketing efforts include site visitation, membership growth and site conversion, and these data points are split into old members, new members, aging members to track behavior. Cost per customer acquisition is also a key metric. "And the best predictor of the cost information that we have 'day one' conversion. So I advertise to a new member. You click. You come in. You buy. So we have a thing called 'day one' conversion metric."

Ballantyne continues, "I also have qualitative KPIs. I have customer health, which is measuring overall satisfaction. I have net promoter score, which we look at on a monthly basis across multiple segments. And I have prospect metrics. And of course things like brand awareness, consideration and preference."

Marketing is front and center of the business. Ballantyne claims that half of the agenda of a board meeting is spent on marketing. "This is the beauty of the board. We have a fantastically supportive advisory type board to keep us on the straight and narrow. But I have a weekly tracker that would make you blind. It's got numbers, and it shows the cohorts and the break even. We get into even that with the board ... They want to know that I'm spending the money efficiently, effectively, and on the right things."

"We've actually slowed our board down as opposed to them slowing us down because we want focus," according to Ballantyne. "If they had their druthers, we'd be in China and Japan. Guys, let's get the US scaling. Let's get Europe going."

Having come from big corporations to Fab, Ballantyne is looking forward to building scale. "I've been in the scaled companies, but what the big scale ones I think lack is the flexibility of something like we have. We have processes when we need them, not for process sake. The big guys are overly processed ... I think we're bringing the best practices and leaving the ones out we don't need.

Summary

While KIND and Fab are two entirely different consumer-facing businesses, they demonstrate some commonalities in terms of running lean and mean, attracting a highly passionate workforce, and being able to write their own rules as the business grows. In fact, while both of these CMOs bring years of traditional marketing experience to their organizations, they seem to revel in having a blank sheet of paper on which to create a winning team and a winning marketing strategy for the business.

5

The Next-Stage CMO

As start-ups evolve, it's likely that these organizations' marketing needs also evolve and morph, as has been the case with the examples in this chapter. In all cases, these CMOs have replaced the function head in their companies as the business has grown and as the marketing needs changed.

Bazaarvoice

ERIN NELSON, CMO, BAZAARVOICE

Prior to joining Bazaarvoice in November 2010 as its CMO, Nelson served as SVP and CMO for Dell Inc., and in 2010, the Advertising Federation of America honored Nelson's distinguished career and inducted her into The Advertising Hall of Achievement for demonstrating the power of ideals-led branding. She also has worked at P&G, PepsiCo and AT Kearney.

The *Wall Street Journal* reported Bazaarvoice's success in an article posted on May 24, 2012. With the headline "Bazaarvoice, One of 2012's Best IPOs, to Buy Rival," the article read: "The social world is abuzz with deal making. Bazaarvoice, a company that works on branding and marketing information for clients by tapping social media sites for direct responses, is spending $151.9 million in cash and stock to purchase competitor PowerReviews Inc.. Bazaarvoice went public in February and is up over 60 percent since then, making it the fifth-best performer among IPOs this year."[1]

---

1   Benoit, D. 2012. Bazaarvoice, One of 2012's Best IPOs, to Buy Rival. *Wall Street Journal*. [Online, May 24, 2012]. Available at: http://blogs.wsj.com/deals/2012/05/24/bazaarvoice-one-of-2012s-best-ipos-to-buy-rival [accessed: October 20, 2012].

As Bazaarvoice goes from strength to strength, its marketing has done likewise under the leadership of Erin Nelson who joined the organization in November 2010, replacing her predecessor, founding CMO Sam Decker who was the third employee to join the company in 2005. As Nelson reminisced, "I think what was different about his regime and focus and mine was that Sam is a total entrepreneur-make-stuff-out-of-stuff-that-doesn't-even-exist, and he did a phenomenal job for the first phase of the company. I think what was required for the next phase was we need to actually globally expand. We need to find our way into new channels. We need to think differently about product innovations. We need to build a much more kind of evocative strategic brand, and so I think it was potentially kind of a different flavor, a different type of CMO that was required. And it's one of the most interesting CMO jobs I think you can have because you're marketing to marketers."

Nelson thinks back on how she came to the company. "So I had been in marketing business development and sales for the majority of my career, and the last 11 years of it were spent at Dell. The first years of my career I was at P&G, PepsiCo and AT Kearney, and what I was recognizing at Dell was that I was on a pretty accelerated path there. I was the fastest person to rise from director to SVP. I was the youngest person ever on the ELT [executive leadership team], and so I achieved some pretty awesome success at Dell by the time I was 39. And one of the things that I had just started to recognize was that I had been there for a fairly long time, but I thought I'm still pretty young and I think I've still got a couple of waves left in my career."

So Nelson thought about what next, and as she did, she recognized that if the Internet was the major wave of business in the 1990s, then social was the current wave. "And I decided this is so big and so huge that I want to actually be more actively engaged and be a part of that."

Joining Bazaarvoice 18 months prior being interviewed for this book, Nelson recollects her early days. She inherited "an entrepreneurial start-up team, and there were a lot of folks that had been with the business for a number of years and they had been more like generalist marketers because they had to be. So a really dedicated team, but what we had to build were some capabilities and special teams that we didn't have. So there has been a lot of growth. It has more than doubled, and it's not just about size. We actually went and found new capabilities, so we just hired, as an example, someone who really specializes in digital demand generation marketing communications." Nelson adds that she hired someone who had been a fixture in the PR and agency world for a number of years to run branding communications, and she and her team built an entire solutions marketing team that didn't exist before. "So in addition to just getting larger, we went and found some terrific areas of leadership and functional capability that we needed."

Out of an entire workforce of some 850 people, Nelson's team, which is marketing and inside sales, is 110 strong split 50/50 between the two disciplines, and she has five direct reports, a bit different to her 4,000-strong team while at Dell. And her responsibilities include all of the communications function—PR, analyst PR, analyst relations, media relations and internal communications; all of advertising and demand generation, including the sales piece of the organization that drives demand generation; solutions marketing which in turn drives product innovation; line marketing with the business units; marketing operations and CRM; and analytics.

Despite being thrown into the deep end [see onboarding in Chapter 2], Nelson was focused and kicked off an initiative literally in her first 30 days to define "who we are, why we matter, really defining our overall brand platform and strategy. I don't think that was always clear to our CMO target ... what's our purpose, why does that matter, how do we emotionally connect with our target, how to we articulate our points of view ... So that was incredibly important because it was foundational."

Nelson continues, "The second thing that was incredibly important was identifying and solving for the gaps and capabilities of the opportunities to augment the team's capability. So we really focused on 'let's build the brand and let's build the team.' Then once we had the team in order and the brand platform, you can start taking that to the next level."

One of the challenges Nelson encountered was that of scale and size when she was used to the seemingly infinite resources of Dell. "The challenge we've always had and always will have is the bandwidth and firepower to execute all of the things that we know we need to do." But Nelson is enthusiastic about her team and her agency partners.

Her peer relationships are important too. Nelson reports to the CEO and sits on the company's executive committee, but she counts her closest peers as the COO, her counterpart for the business unit, and her CFO.

Nelson has done a lot of augmenting the analytics space. "You never have enough data about your customers or the market, so we did two things right away. First, we actually kicked off a market sizing analysis and strategy that we'd never done before to really understand the market space and the white space … The second thing we did … is get a lot more analytics about our clients, our customers … We're a social company that generates unbelievable amounts of data, so in terms of preference and desire, we have tons and tons of this awesome data. And we actually started packaging it and utilizing it in a different way, so we now publish a quarterly thought-leadership piece that's called 'The Conversation Index,' and it's about the themes of the data that we're seeing."

Going forward, Nelson has a couple of key areas of focus. "The biggest two for me are going to be market expansion. We already operate in a couple of continents heavily—North America and Europe. What we don't have is a meaningful business in either Asia or Latin America, so that is number one priority on our list right now. How do we actually globally expand? The second piece is how do we identify new ways to drive value in our market and new markets to go serve. So we're launching into the small and medium business segment of the market where we haven't been before. And we're looking right now at our whole innovation roadmap on how we can really start to drive value for CMOs on the brand side … Another piece is that we want to obviously go drive tremendous amounts of awareness and consideration growth for the brand. We've experienced great success but there's so much more to be done, and so it's really turning up the volume."

Havaiana

CARLOS ZEPEDA, VP, MARKETING, ALPARGATAS USA/HAVAIANAS

Carlos Zepeda assumed the role as the lead marketer for the Havaianas brand, in the US in September 2012. Previously, he held multiple director and senior manager roles within PepsiCo, and prior to that, he worked in management consultancy with Ernst and Young, and Peppers and Rogers Group.

Like Nelson, Carlos Zepeda was recruited from the outside the company into an upgraded marketing role. The process was a long one—four months—and he started in early

September 2012. He reports to the president of the US operation, who in turn reports into the president of the sandals business unit of parent company Alpargatas. Founded in 1907, Alpargatas is the producer of two global brands — Havaianas in Brazil and Topper in Argentina. The company also manufactures Dupé, Rainha, Mizuno, Timberland and Séte Léguas, known for their design and technology.

Zepeda claims his was a very structured and methodical onboarding process led by the outgoing president who had originally interviewed him, and who was being promoted and sent back to Brazil. He inherited a new president who was the former head of finance.

Getting started, Zepeda did three things:

1. Scan the business, including the brand, the organizational charts, the agency partners, finding out who had influence and power in the organization.

2. Identify the definition of success between the different stakeholders. "Some people tell me 'we have to increase awareness,' some say 'we have to double the business in a couple of years,' some others say 'we've got to make sure we get the best people,' or 'we have to open stores,' and the story goes on.

3. "Let the facts mingle with my gut" — so he started getting acquainted with the brand tracking, the budget, the people, and so on. "I think the challenge is that sometimes we get attached to it [preconceived notion] and we start working on things without putting them in context."

Zepeda inherited a small team that had previously reported to an interim marketing head, a group of people trying to increase brand awareness and do "cool things" that would get noticed by the press and drive impressions for the brand. "It was a combination of a lot of paid media, very static paid media like print, with a lot of PR activity. It was like 'steak and sizzle.' The 'steak' was the print advertising, and the 'sizzle' was the PR. But it was 80 percent 'steak'."

So Zepeda is embarking on a journey to increase the accountability of marketing and to demonstrate how marketing can contribute to the growth agenda. "I'm introducing a different context for the marketing activities around the path to purchase versus being solely focused on awareness. It's more focused on having consumers navigate along this path: from awareness to consideration to eventually becoming a customer. Awareness is important, but conversion is as if not more important," he says.

In addition to inheriting a small team internally, Zepeda also inherited a small roster of agency partners in digital, PR, media and experiential. The global creative agency is based in Brazil. When he joined the company, he undertook agency review across the US partners and determined that the only discipline he would put out to bid would be the experiential piece.

Planning for the future, Zepeda is committed to changing the KPIs of marketing. There had been no strict connection between the awareness tracking and the sales. So, while he and his president come from different worlds, their thoughts on metrics seem to converge. According to Zepeda, "When we were writing the strategy for next year, he was writing the strategy for the business and I was writing the strategy for the marketing. We went through a similar process and we were sharing notes, and we said, 'wait a second—we're talking about the same thing.' So we merged business and marketing and now we have one strategy."

Zepeda's definition of success is now much more multi-dimensional. It includes market share—not just brand awareness but awareness that drives growth. His definition also includes increasing awareness, but instead of total awareness, he has selected awareness for his cohort, his specific target audience. The third aspect of success is based on the campaign—campaign recall, impact and response. Finally, in his "last bucket," he includes imagery and personality, and consumer engagement metrics. This includes brand imagery and personality scores. At the end of the day, awareness needs to mean something to consumers. He says, "Those metrics are now what I call a center of gravity. Everyone is connected to those metrics. And there's no going back because it is about accountability." Ultimately, he's looking to create a new metric—"lifetime value"—a combination of customer loyalty over a period of years based on purchase projections.

He continues, "There's a difference between measuring and being accountable for the measurement. A lot of the things I'm selecting to be measured have been measured before, but they've been hidden in reports. No one was taking responsibility or ownership of them … I think sometimes metrics are so aggregated that it's hard to make them actionable."

To deliver against these KPIs, Zepeda is looking to improve integration across channels, especially digital and social. In his opinion, there are five aspects he's focused on to achieve that:

1. define brand promise and share across all teams and stakeholders;

2. create the right team structure to drive message consistency and speed;

3. create rich and multi-level shared metrics system (from business to consumer engagement);

4. let ideas and brand conversations naturally integrate initiatives;

5. utilize a cross-functional brand touch point dashboard to manage brand conversations.

ARM Holdings

IAN DREW, EVP, MARKETING AND BUSINESS DEVELOPMENT, ARM

Ian Drew was appointed as EVP Strategy in August 2011, having previously been EVP of marketing since 2008. He joined ARM in 2005 as VP segment marketing. Previously, he worked at Intel for 14 years in various senior management roles around the world including Asia, Europe and the US.

ARM Holdings is a British multinational semiconductor and software design company headquartered in Cambridge, England. Its largest business is in processors, although it also designs software development tools under the RealView and Keil brands, systems and platforms, system-on-a-chip infrastructure and software. It is considered to be market dominant in the field of mobile phone chips and is arguably the best-known of the "Cambridge Cluster" of high-tech companies. The company was founded in 1990 as Advanced RISC Machines—a joint venture between Acorn Computers, Apple and VLSI Technology. ARM

Holdings has a primary listing on the London Stock Exchange and is a constituent of the FTSE 100 Index, and it has a secondary listing on NASDAQ.

Ian Drew joined ARM Holdings in 2005 as VP of Segment Marketing. He was appointed as EVP of Strategy in August, 2011, having previously been EVP—Marketing since July 2008. Much of what he did in marketing he's taking into his new role, in which he has replaced someone who had moved into another job at ARM.

According to Drew, "When I first came in, three things struck me. One was that we needed to get a lot closer to the social media side. We were doing PR in the old fashioned way and putting out press releases and doing [trade] shows. One of the big things was, we did a lot more work in social media ahead of the curve that you're seeing now." For example, Drew talks about ARM's social media training for its engineers. "So you'll find our blogs and tweets are really written by engineers, not by marketing dweebs," he says.

Drew continues, "The second priority was thinking more not just of our semi conductor partners but also our original equipment manufacturers (OEMs), the software guys, how to build the whole ecosystem. How you get in a win–win situation with them. We worked with the browser companies; we worked with the software companies and we helped launch Androids. There were lots of things that we did that were fairly logical, but at the time were quite revolutionary … The third area was around a competitive program. In marketing, it's easy to pick your competitors. In ARM, we picked Intel which at the time was pretty radical."

Drew has morphed his team to accomplish these goals. "I needed some young, vibrant people to come in and tell us about social media. I needed some people in software who understood software and weren't hardware guys. I needed some people with new business experience, and so I brought some people in, I promoted some people, and I kept some people where they were. But you have to create a team that really is a team rather than a set of individuals." His direct reports grew to six "because we were actually doing more," but the overall size of his team, at 80–90 people, stayed relatively the same. And he changed his agency, moving from a traditional PR agency to a non-traditional social media agency.

His biggest people challenge is motivating them when he's not there. "You have to share a vision. You have to communicate regularly. My phone bill is always one of the highest around. I'm not a great email writer. I like sharing visions and helping people, and trying to set objectives that they feel are achievable but will grow and reward them."

Drew is aghast that a chief marketing role would not have responsibility for PR, especially since ARM uses PR and social as its main marketing channel. "I think that increasingly the ability to get life-size, page-two, column six in a magazine has gone away now. It's how do you get into people's psyche by doing the right thing and connecting to the right people. And that means social media." His additional responsibilities include segment marketing (vertical marketing), business development, new business, software relations, analyst relations, competitive analysis and "black ops," which is ARM's term for special programs. And he works very closely with sales.

In fact, his closest peers include sales, finance and HR. Drew's team manages internal communications in terms of messaging, but HR controls it in terms of putting the processes in place.

Drew reports to the COO officially, but he has reported to the CEO previously. "At the moment, it just depends on who's doing what and when," he said.

As he took on his new role in 2011, Drew outlines some of the new challenges he faced. "How do you motivate a team that has been recently successful to go and climb some bigger hills? How do you go and grow the breadth of the company, where you need to expand to, and how do you do it profitably? How do you enable the company to grow? And what's the long-term, three- to five-year vision of where we need to be?" But it's not just about the business goals. He adds, "How do you make sure all of the executives stand up and say the right messages at the right time? How do you make sure you're not reactive to your competitors, that you're proactive instead?"

Drew is proud of ARM's culture: "I'd define the culture as typically British. I'd define it as making sure our partners are successful. It's very much a part of our partnership model—working with lots of companies to help define a spectrum of differentiation that provides good value to the end user."

Going forward, Drew is focused on taking ARM's marketing to a new level to achieve new goals. "I think for ARM, it's getting people to use the Internet everywhere, low power enablement of all this new Internet technology. And the starting of things like 'the Internet of things,' (IOT), all of this through connected Internet devices."

ServiceSource

CHRISTINE HECKART, CMO, SERVICESOURCE

Christine Heckart assumed the role of CMO at ServiceSource in July 2012. She also sits on the board of LAM Research. Prior to her current role, Heckart was CMO of NetApp, general manager of marketing & ecosystem for Microsoft, and VP and CMO of Juniper Networks.

ServiceSource is the global leader in recurring revenue management and works with some of the world's most successful companies to maximize subscription, maintenance and support revenue, improve customer retention and increase business predictability and insight. With over a decade of experience focused exclusively in growing recurring revenue, the organization's services and applications are based on proven best practices and global benchmarks. ServiceSource is headquartered in San Francisco, and has over $7 billion under management for customers in more than 150 countries and 40 languages. It has regional offices in Kuala Lumpur, Malaysia; Singapore; Dublin, Ireland; Liverpool, England; Denver, CO and Nashville, TN.

When Christine Heckart, ServiceSource's new CMO, was interviewed for this book, she had been in her post for only three months. And although she had been recruited by a search firm, she had a previous relationship with several of the executives on the team. "Being somewhat of a known entity can have some real advantages in terms of both getting an opportunity and being successful in an opportunity," she said.

In her first 90 days, Heckart suggested that any new job in the first several months is the easiest time. "Whatever drama is going on in the organization is not your drama. You're in learning mode and you're trying to listen to everybody's perspective, what's working, what's not working, what's missing, and that's always where I start." She continued, "I try to talk to all of the key stakeholders and depending on the size of the department, lots and lots of people in the department."

While Heckart's onboarding process seemed fairly straightforward, she quickly found that within her first six weeks, "there was a small matter of getting a major launch out the door—a big whirlwind, not great timing. But that can be good because you get to really evaluate people. You see exactly what's going on, who's good, who's not, and you can be blunt about it." The downside though is inheriting the process. "When you're dropped into something big that's already in play, you can't influence it all that much by that point, and you're stuck with it."

Heckart did manage to intercept a lot of the messaging which, she says, six weeks before the end of a launch at a bigger company would have been impossible. Because ServiceSource is a smaller company and everything was in turmoil, she was able to make some decisions. "The bad news is that I'm doing it on very limited information. There are some good sides too. You're learning really fast. You're getting a fast assessment. You're able to make a contribution pretty quickly. You're able to get to know people pretty quickly, a little bit of bonding because you're going through something big. So that can be the upside to it."

The good news is that the launch went well. According to Heckart, "I would say that it was a really heroic effort by a lot of people in the marketing team. What it points to is their agility and being able to have somebody brand new come on and look through all of this stuff, make changes very late in the game, and some of those changes would have been made anyway. I mean, this stuff wasn't locked down, but it points to a very agile marketing department."

Heckart's predecessor moved into a strategy role within the company, leaving the CMO role vacant for six months before Heckart joined. As well, there was a VP role to fill, but because the executive team wanted the new CMO to be able to fill it, that went vacant for six months as well. And some of the people who had reported to the previous VP also had left. "So you walk in and you're starting with this organization that's kind of gutted," Heckart said. "A lot of times you're starting with an organization that is not in great health to begin with."

In terms of building peer relationships, sales is a key discipline for Heckart, and developing a tight relationships with IT is becoming increasingly important too, "because so much of what you want to try to get done, not just inside marketing, but inside the company as a whole, can have an IT component, and if you happen to be marketing to the technical community like I have done in most of my jobs, then the IT person is really a good representative of your customer base so you can use them in your own marketing and so forth." Heckart counts HR as key as well, and finance, obviously.

Heckart's responsibilities are "all marketing" including field marketing, PR, internal communications in partnership with HR, product and solution marketing (which is not part of the business units at ServiceSource), and all traditional disciplines such as web, demand generation and so on. As well, Heckart is responsible for marketing operations, analytics and analyst relations.

Heckart claims that, "The company itself is in the state of a big transition which is why they brought me in. ServiceSource is going from selling primarily professional services to selling the Cloud application. So what it needs from marketing is very different going forward. The charter for marketing itself will change. There will be brand new things added in and there will be parts of the department that really need to be built up so that product marketing, for example, has to be added in because there really wasn't product before. There was a whole professional service solution, but there wasn't a hard product with features and capabilities and there wasn't a launch process where every quarter you're launching new stuff."

So Heckart has her work cut out for her going forward. She will need to add, create or re-engineer a formal launch process, field marketing, demand generation and thought leadership initiatives. And she's trying to intercept the next budgeting cycle in order to obtain the investment required to achieve certain priorities. "There are some people that have a pretty big appetite for doing more awareness marketing and brand building, but as you know, it can take some money to do that," she says.

When asked how marketing is viewed by the ServiceSource board, Heckart replies, "I would say that marketing is very visible by the board. The CEO is a huge champion of marketing. He's got a big appetite. He's a big believer. He thinks marketing is what will propel the company forward, which is, you know, very nice. Very refreshing. He wants to make more investments in marketing, so as a result, there is a lot more visibility on the board for both the challenges that the department has and needs to address as well as the contributions that marketing makes."

Summary

These CMOs provide a range of experiences as their companies have continued to grow and branch out into new products and/or services. In all cases, the CMOs are benefiting from the heightened interest that both the CEOs and boards are giving to the discipline, and marketing is becoming more pivotal to each organization's business development and sales function.

6

The New Centralized CMO

It has not gone unnoticed that several quite large organizations have heightened the importance of marketing as a more central role above and beyond business units and brand categories. Among them are Johnson & Johnson, Colgate-Palmolive, BASF and Georgia–Pacific—all for different but related reasons.

Johnson & Johnson

MICHAEL SNEED, VP, GLOBAL CORPORATE AFFAIRS, JOHNSON & JOHNSON

Michael Sneed is VP, global corporate affairs for Johnson & Johnson, with primary responsibility for the corporation's global marketing and communications functions. He joined J&J in 1983 and has held marketing and general management roles in Europe, North America, Asia Pacific and Latin America.

Michael Sneed assumed the new position of VP, global corporate affairs, for Johnson & Johnson in January 2012 after having been with the company since 1983 in a variety of marketing and general management positions. In the new role, he has primary responsibility for the corporation's global marketing and communications functions.

"When J&J looked at the landscape of reputation, communication, equity and stakeholder alignment, it became clear that all of these things were kind of colliding, and we had operated those things fairly separately in the past. I think that in different times, that was perfectly okay. But now with the amount of media that's out there, I think that with the scrutiny on large companies in general, and the fact that our stakeholders have evolved and changed over time, it became clear that we just needed a more cohesive approach to all of these areas, and to do it in a way that we could have a coherent strategy. I think that was the impetus behind it," reasoned Sneed.

Secondly, because the role was fairly broad, the J&J management believed that they needed someone who really understood the organization, the culture and the players. Sneed fit the bill.

"J&J tended to keep itself in the background and really wanted the operating companies to speak and wanted the focus to be on the brands. That model served us very well. But the environment has changed and if you're not out there telling your story, other people will tell it for you," according to Sneed.

What were some of the first things he did? "I restructured the organization to focus on a couple of key areas. We have a number of external stakeholders that are really important to us so we needed a plan and a group that would focus on them. The second important stakeholder for us was our employees. Given how engaged they are with J&J and their passion about the credo, at the enterprise level we really didn't do a lot in terms of communicating to them as J&J employees, outside of their operating companies. We want them to understand what's happening across the breadth of J&J, but also we really want them to be ambassadors ... Those are probably the two most substantive changes I made when I first came in," said Sneed.

There have been some early successes, too. According to Sneed, "We've definitely changed the dialogue between the enterprise and the employees. There are some small initiatives, but they do matter, such as just getting our CEO in a forum where he can blog a couple times a week, which some people thought would be too risky. It's been great to see the employee comments. You can tell the level of engagement is just so much higher. And on the communication front, we've packaged our information to be a lot more accessible to our employees and external stakeholders ... We were inundating people with emails from corporate about this and that; 90 percent of it had no relevance to the individual. So we worked with IT because virtually every operating company thought the thing that they were focused on was the most important thing in the world. And now we put everything together in a 'package' with an emphasis on using pictures and video."

Sneed is responsible for all disciplines that are marketing or communications-oriented including external stakeholder communication, employee communication, corporate philanthropy, advertising and media (including social media), PR, public affairs, metrics and analytics. Government affairs and investor relations are outside his scope, but he works closely with those teams. The two areas that seem to be going through the most change are social media and analytics.

Sneed is circumspect about social media: "It is an increased risk, but you'd be surprised how customers, consumers and patients give you so much credit just for listening. Even if something doesn't go right, the fact that you're taking the time to listen and in some cases apologize or make things right, that goes almost as far as doing things right the first time. It's really amazing ... I think we've gotten a lot more comfortable with that dialogue," he said.

The analytics piece seems to be work in progress. Sneed is a huge believer in the concept of net promoter score, having built it into the business metrics for the Vision Care business of which he was company group chairman before taking on his current role.

When asked to describe his job in one sentence, Sneed would say, "My job is to ensure that J&J's reputation continues to grow over time." He added that "reputation" is a loaded word, and that 95 percent of what makes up reputation is what the company and its employees do. "J&J is a great company, but with that greatness carries a tremendous amount of responsibility, and in today's environment, there's a tremendous amount of scrutiny."

Colgate–Palmolive

NIGEL BURTON, CMO, COLGATE–PALMOLIVE

Nigel Burton joined Colgate in 1979 in its UK marketing department. He was promoted to his current role as CMO in 2011. In between, he has served in a number of management and marketing roles including general manager for Colgate US, VP of marketing for the company in Canada, and general manager of Colgate–Palmolive in Spain.

Whereas reputation was the core driver behind creating a centralized marketing leader role at J&J, Colgate–Palmolive shared the importance of reputation as a driver along with building centralized competencies and capabilities to further contribute to brand health. According to Nigel Burton, Colgate's first overall CMO, "First, the outside world was moving faster than we were ... Secondly, we felt that there were so many aspects about digital that were global in terms of capabilities, this was one area where we really couldn't afford to lead it in 228 different locations, even though we had a history of allowing a lot of local and regional input and decision-making in order that the businesses were obligated to have accountability for results. We're a global company—we were actually one of the first companies I think that really got its hands around the idea of global marketing and global brands, but we needed to build digital capability centrally. There are so many things that are more empowering, more efficient, more effective, if you look at it from a global capability."

Like Sneed, Burton has had a long career at Colgate. Joining in 1979, he held a series of positions of increasing responsibility until, in 2005, he was promoted to president of the Global Oral Care business. He was promoted to CMO in 2011, where he is responsible for all of the global categories and brands, as well as global insights, global advertising, digital groups and shopper marketing on a worldwide basis. He also has integrated marketing communications, of which brand PR is part, but he does not "own" corporate communications or company PR. And packaging sits as a stand-alone function because it involves the design piece as well as the engineering piece, so from a matrix perspective, it works with the marketing and supply chain teams respectively.

Before Burton's appointment, all marketing efforts were driven by the teams within the individual brands. "Colgate's view was that we didn't want a marketing leader absent the business because it could risk becoming disconnected, and not have enough impetus or ability to actually change what's going on," he said. "So we were waiting. We wanted it to be done in a way that had credibility within the organization, for someone who knew the essence and what goes on day to day."

Burton's priorities when he took on the position were, first, to get back up to speed or get to know the categories other than oral care. His second order of business was related to getting out into some of the markets with a different set of eyes. He had been to visit all of Colgate's main subsidiaries and markets, but according to Burton, "I needed to go and see them in the context of our business overall."

Third on his list was talking to the other leaders in the organization—the business and divisional leaders, as well as the other functional leaders such as technology, supply chain, IT—his stakeholders as he calls them. The fourth priority was taking all of that into account and to put together a two- to three-year agenda for the fundamentals to attack.

Burton reports to the two chief operating officers (COOs) of the company: one who is responsible for the other global functions, and the other who is responsible for the geographies. There is a slight twist in that the COO who is responsible for the functions also has some of the geographies.

Burton works in a matrix structure. His team is comprised of category heads of marketing representing the business side related to the global categories, and leaders of various marketing components, such as global advertising, global insights and so on. He also has a marketing HR specialist that works with him via a dotted line relationship, as well as a marketing training head.

Since taking on the role, Burton has established five platforms in the organization's marketing agenda. "The first item is around the global categories and growth and how we optimize growth relative to resources. The second platform is about improving brand health. We've been lucky enough to inherit some great brands that previous generations have created for us. We've got to pass it on to the next generation in better shape than we inherited them, so this is all about how we continue to have a brand focus and a focus on brand health."

"The third area is what we call IMC, integrated marketing and communications which, in the old days, would be called great advertising, but is now called effective communication across all of the touch points including digital, packaging and shopper marketing. The fourth bucket would be innovation, and how we continue to optimize our innovation with a few to more breakthrough as opposed to incremental." The fifth platform is around the people, the talent (see Chapter 10).

BASF

JACK ARMSTRONG, DIRECTOR, MARKETING COMMUNICATIONS NORTH AMERICA, BASF

Joining BASF in 1989, Jack Armstrong took on his current role as director of marketing communications for North America in April 2011. Previous posts include general management and regional marketing roles for several BASF businesses, with postings in Sao Paolo, Brazil; Brussels, Belgium; Texas and New Jersey.

From two very big B2C brands headquartered in the US, BASF provides a contrast. Although BASF does have a B2C portfolio, it is primarily a B2B business, and it's based in Germany. Jack Armstrong, Director of Marketing Communications for North America, took on his newly-created role to provide a central conduit to the company's diversified marketing efforts. He joined BASF in 1989 and, with a degree in chemical engineering, he moved around the organization with posts in Sao Paulo, Brussels and New Jersey where he is currently located.

To provide a sense of just how diverse BASF's marketing efforts are, "We probably have 20 independent chains of sales people and sometimes even within the same industry, they don't know each other," according to Armstrong. "If it's, say, construction, because construction is such a big part of our business, there's the world of concrete additives in cement, and those sales people in those channels are so completely different to those selling insulation or paint to Sherwin Williams and Benjamin Moore."

Armstrong continued, "We found that it was very difficult to have one marketing department for the whole corporation or even one marketing department for just one division because the in-market attributes are just so big. So I think that when you're in a huge multinational kind of conglomerate like BASF, you have to realize that we're going to let everybody do what's right for their industry for their niche, but at the same time, there was never any kind of steering the ship from the top."

That's where Armstrong came in when he was appointed in April, 2011, which was driven by the desire at board level to build brand equity in markets where the BASF brand strength and recognition were less than in its native European market. To provide some context, according to Armstrong, BASF unaided brand awareness in Europe is 30–40 percent. In North America, unaided brand awareness for Dow and DuPont is also 30–40 percent, but for BASF, it's more like 10 percent. So, he said, "From 2005 to 2008, everybody at the board level really started to see there was reason and synergy to start adopting a global messaging structure."

Armstrong's team still supports each of the divisions, helping each business to craft their market and communications strategies, but at the same time they establish some kind of commonality so that there's a thread that ties everything together from a corporate positioning perspective.

This is no mean feat given that the BASF Corporation in North America is really a collection of acquisitions coming on board since 1985. "Even through the mid-1990s, we were just getting everybody on the same enterprise management systems, the same accounting systems and the same email system. I'd say it was really only the early 2000s when we were really able to start having everybody brand with the BASF brand, and create an understanding of what the brand stood for and its attributes," Armstrong said. "Then in 2008, we decided to start doing global advertising—before it had been advertising just for Europe, South America, Asia or North America."

Given the diversity of the BASF business, Armstrong likens the BASF business as a kind of "innovation engine inside their customers' businesses or products." "So what we realized was that if we don't take control somewhat of the high-level messaging, then nobody's going to realize that BASF is really 'the Intel inside' of the company, so to speak. That was really the goal."

As a result, Armstrong has been working to develop a BASF brand innovation culture. "We have a matrix organization, so the 15 business lines have the profit and loss (P&L) responsibilities. Then, in a parallel organization, we have competency centers, so we have treasury, engineering, production, safety, sustainability, HR and communications. And each of the business units, where they sit in a geographic region, has a local infrastructure to support those 15 divisions." Armstrong continued, "We'd gone back and forth organizationally between marketing communications being independent and embedded in each of the business units versus pulling it out of the business unit and having it sit across the corporate competency functions. But we realized that if it's embedded in the business unit, they get so siloed, and they don't really carry the corporate message."

So Armstrong has his tentacles in each of the 15 divisions, and what he's trying to establish is a center for marketing excellence. One big area he sees for improvement is the area of metrics in terms of injecting a degree of objectivity from the center and some common KPIs as well as some additional analytics around the digital space. Additionally, he sees corporate sustainability as an enterprise-wide platform, as well as internal marketing and internal communications. To establish some consistency across the organization, he and his team have created a score card for divisions as well to assess, for example, "marketing assets and collateral by division, brand compliancy, website appearance and number of websites, tracking website traffic, etc."

There is a "slight policing aspect" to the role in terms of making sure that each division is doing its utmost to be "on brand," but Armstrong also makes an offer to pay for some initiatives since many of the divisions are so budget conscious that it is sometimes difficult to get them to invest in checking brand awareness. "I started to instill the philosophy that BASF is the mother ship brand and is really only as strong as the component brands underneath. Unless we know where the component brands are, we can't track their health and their awareness as linked to the overall BASF mother-brand."

PR is used extensively by BASF as well. "So if we're members of key trade associations—we need to not only advertise on their websites and be in their newsletters, but we also need our people on the panels and committees, and every time there's a relevant conference, we need to be on those programs. Having our people media trained and being on point is a necessity."

Armstrong is an advocate of earned media. "When you don't have a lot of money to spend, you have to use a little more ingenuity in terms of using the web and social media, and distilling the complicated geeky nerdy chemical stuff up to really high-level speaking points around benefits, attributes and 'what's in it for me.' At the end of the day, a sale is a sale," he said.

Contrary to anyone else interviewed for the book, Armstrong reports to the chief communications officer (CCO) who in turn reports to the CEO in North America. He also has a dotted line to the global head of communications based in Germany, along with his counterparts in Asia, South America and Europe.

His North American territory covers everything from Panama north. When asked who led the role before he was appointed, it's astonishing to learn that the role was traditionally filled by an advertising agency executive out of New York, which churned on a regular basis. His position sat empty for nine months because management couldn't fill it in the same way as before. So it was decided to appoint from the inside—someone that would bring organizational network and understanding, and who had illustrated competencies in marketing, communications and business.

When he started, he set some priorities for his first 90 days. "One was to earn the trust and credibility around the vision that we could do some really great things together. The department had a low image. We were seen as tactical only, so there was some repositioning and reinvigorating that needed to be done. And I needed to resolve some organizational issues so I made some changes and we shuffled people and brought on a couple of additional people. I also spent some time to talk with and listen to the 15 business unit leaders as well as the executive leaders."

BASF - Corporate Communications Organizational Chart

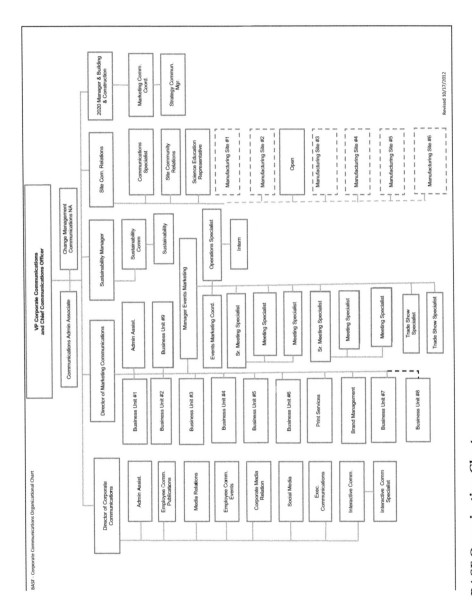

Figure 6.1   BASF Organization Chart

Armstrong inherited a set of responsibilities, but he also "reached out and grabbed stuff like social marketing and Internet management." He has established a leader board of metrics by division which has, in turn, created some internal rivalry via "the embarrassment factor." He consolidated agencies and printing firms to achieve some economies of scale—a process that had been started before he came into the role, and he took ownership of the trade show, meeting and events group which has given him and his team a great platform for messaging, whether they're handling an internal employee meeting, sales meeting or external event. This latter team has 25 full-time employees but at times ladders up to 100 depending on conferencing needs, and in 2011, the team planned 358 meetings, which was set to increase considerably in 2012.

He and his team also are big proponents of cross-selling across the enterprise. "We did a big survey where we saw 80 percent of our customers buy from only one division. We recognized an opportunity, so we launched our Vision 2020 Program aiming to generate 10 percent new sales just through cross-divisional collaboration—just the same customers that we've always had but letting those customers know that we have 14 other divisions … That's been really fun for me, and it's enlightening and invigorating for the employees because they learn about the whole other part of BASF they never knew."

Armstrong has achieved much in his first few months, but he isn't stopping there. "My next vision for 2013 is how I can take what we're doing in marketing communication to the next level via interactivity tools with our customers, looking at how a company like BASF can add value in the day-to-day life of our customers and distribution channel partners," said Armstrong.

Georgia–Pacific

DOUWE BERGSMA, CMO, GEORGIA–PACIFIC

Douwe Bergsma joined Georgia–Pacific as the first CMO in 2011. He began his career in marketing at P&G in his home country, the Netherlands, and for 19 years enjoyed several marketing positions there in Europe and North America, most recently heading marketing and innovation for the Pringles brand in the Americas.

From publicly-quoted multinationals to a privately-held, largely-North American enterprise, Georgia–Pacific appointed its first overall CMO in March, 2011. Douwe Bergsma was head-hunted from the outside—he had been leading marketing for P&G's Pringles brand in North America, having been with the company since 1991. And from a digital perspective, he is in the unique position of moving from www.pg.com to www.gp.com so he says, "Every now and then, people are still confused by this."

In joining Georgia–Pacific, Bergsma consistently talks about creating some "restless discontent" in the organization. He admits that when he joined the organization, "Most everything was good, but we have the opportunity to become even better or even great."

Bergsma speaks to Georgia–Pacific's strengths in asset utilization and retail customers, but how do companies grow beyond those two strengths? "It's typically innovation and brand building. And I think that's when Georgia–Pacific realized that they still had room to grow in those two areas, and they staffed up significantly in both areas … I think that's when they realized that in order to accelerate driving brand-building capabilities, it would be beneficial to have someone focus on it in the form of a CMO. They did not have a CMO before this. Instead, the marketing and brand-building capabilities were spread across different functions, brands and categories."

Georgia–Pacific's onboarding process for Bergsma was extensive (see Chapter 2). Above that, Bergsma quickly assimilated with four key peers which he viewed as his internal clients. "I quickly connected with the sales manager for two reasons: 1) I identified that the integration and connection with our sales had opportunity, and 2) from a personal level, he joined the organization three years previously with a similar objective—to build capabilities in the sales area. So he was my predecessor from a capability-building perspective. He also had experience coming from the outside, having a long career elsewhere coming in, building a capability center, and then driving it on the sales. And I was expected to do the same on the marketing side."

Then, Bergsma also connected to the three general managers of the P&Ls: tissue, towel and tabletop. These four were the CMO's internal clients and investors because they were basically funding marketing. The fifth key internal influencer was the finance function which was covered by two departments— economic which covered strategy and business development, and traditional finance.

He described his own team that he inherited as "pretty top heavy" with 11 direct reports and 40 overall. But that has changed. "Now I have 72 people in total with seven directors reporting directly to me." This was not directly attributable to hiring new team members. The training department moved from the sales organization, and some of the growth was driven by adding a new organization. "So we had the three categories and we added a fourth. The biggest growth has been in the area of insights and design because those are also the two areas where we increased our investments and activities significantly over the last two years," said Bergsma.

If he looks at his role, Bergsma basically sees his key responsibilities as being part of the management team, working with his peers to drive the overall business; and as function head of marketing where he has a role for all marketers, including those that don't directly report in to him, but are within the categories and in the brands. As he says, "So they would look to me as their functional manager to coach, direct, enable them to drive marketing better, smarter or faster, and I have my own department, which we call brand acceleration. And that department has a lot of the capabilities centralized."

The groups break down into 1) insights, 2) strategy and analytics, 3) the brand center, and 4) shared brand building services.

1. Within insights, each category has a team and there is a central team that helps with the capabilities across all of the insights people.

2. Within strategy and analytics, all of the organization's analytical capabilities are housed centrally. This includes market mix modeling (MMM) and predictive analytics, and the group also is responsible for integrating business plan processes, looking at how the organization can optimize its processes with sales and marketing partners.

3. The brand center is focused predominantly on the marketing content including equity development, copy development, communication development and communication production. It is this group that interacts with Georgia–Pacific's agency partners, develops the play books and the equity trees, writes the creative briefs, and decides who should be producing the work.

4. Finally, shared brand building services includes media planning and buying—an area that existed but which has been expanded

and more centralized—sustainability, promotions, supplier management, and digital.

Regarding digital, Bergsma admits that Georgia–Pacific's engagement has been historically low, but he also points to the area as one where there is a lot of development work. "We had never done search. There were a few brands that had Facebook pages, but they were predominantly managed by corporate communications and not the brands themselves. So there was a lot of opportunity in the digital space and we started developing some capabilities and hiring folks from the outside to contribute."

Two areas outside of Bergsma's direct control are PR, which sit in corporate communications, and shopper marketing, which is based within the sales organization. That said, there are strong ties to both to ensure connectivity and integration.

While Bergsma admits to the first three months being "like drinking from a fire hose," despite the comprehensive onboarding process, he can point to some early successes. "It so happened that we had a big national business meeting in Orlando in my third month here, so that was a perfect opportunity for me to get on stage and communicate to a few hundred folks what we were going to do and what we were going to focus on. And interestingly enough, I got it 90 percent right because a year later when I had much more time to think things through, the vision hadn't changed all that much. The wording got better, and some things were added, but we're still pursuing and driving the vision we communicated back then. That was job number one."

Simultaneously, he was looking at talent. "I was blessed with the fact that I had a lot of talent in house already, but they weren't necessarily aligned to what they could do best. So I didn't move a lot of folks out, or didn't move a lot of folks in. I just reassigned some folks so it became clearer what to focus on."

Did he have any challenges coming in as its first CMO? Yes, he detailed three:

1. Integration within marketing and across other functions. "A consumer interacts with the brand across the path to purchase. But yet, we are organized by function. We're investing by function, we're measuring by function, and therefore it drives a lot of activities by function. And one of my biggest frustrations was that the sales strategies and plans and activities were kind of developed

in isolation to the brand activities ... So we have now started a journey called integrated business planning," said Bergsma.

2.   The holistic brand approach. "Up until last year [2011], I would say that the marketing plan was predominantly comprised of four elements: very, very heavy on TV, a significant level of shopping marketing, and that was kind of it for most brands. Some of them also had print and maybe some PR activity. But that was about it ... And so we're moving to a more holistic brand approach."

3.   Innovation. "For me, we're making strong progress on product innovation, but there's a lot of opportunity to grow in the area of innovation that doesn't involve an improvement of a physical product attribute ... Some people call it conceptual innovation, commercial innovation, give it a name, but innovation that doesn't necessarily include the change of a product attribute or function."

It would appear that Bergsma has achieved much in a short time to up the organization's marketing game, maybe because Georgia–Pacific prides itself on being entrepreneurial. By Bergsma's own admission, "In our market-based philosophy, we basically expect employees to behave as entrepreneurs within a large corporation. So we hardly talk about leadership. We always talk about principled entrepreneurship. We expect that people first and foremost will act with integrity."

So while change has been embraced largely, Bergsma admits that he needs to try to be disciplined and maybe take a step back and slow it down. "I just had my performance review and one of the things was in capital letters: SLOW DOWN. I interpreted that as providing a better focus because that's what it comes down to. Because you look across the board and you see all these things and you try to address everything, but you have to go as fast as your organization is willing, because otherwise you will lose them," he reasons.

Summary

Four big companies—four new CMO roles created, each for a distinct set of reasons, but also sharing some common drivers which can best be summed up as the following points:

•   As brand has increasingly merged with reputation, many larger organizations recognize the need to centrally manage enterprise-wide reputations above and beyond individual brands' or operating companies' reputations. This convergence has largely been driven by an increased transparency in the marketplace around individual brand ownership, and the growing importance of customer satisfaction.

- Centralization of a higher marketing function can provide many benefits including the achievement of greater economy of scale, setting standards across the enterprise for marketing competencies and capabilities, providing a central resource and learning— particularly for new technologies as they apply to the marketing discipline, and putting greater emphasis on the role marketing has in setting enterprise-wide strategy and achieving enterprise-wide growth.

7

The Evolutionary B2C CMO

In IBM's State of Marketing Survey 2012,[1] its opening gambit states, "Consumers are changing marketing. Today's consumers are well-informed, social media-savvy, and likely have two or more mobile devices. They are more demanding—expecting current and perpetually shifting new channels, such as mobile and social, to deliver an exceptional customer experience." As such, many companies marketing consumer brands are shifting up their marketing capabilities in an effort to revolutionize how they go to market.

YouTube

DANIELLE TIEDT, CMO, YOUTUBE

 **Danielle Tiedt joined YouTube as CMO in February 2012 to play a pivotal role in the organization's next phase of growth. Previously, she was general manager (GM) of Microsoft's Bing, and led the search engine's brand push "Bing is for Doing."**

Danielle Tiedt had been in her CMO role for about 90 days when interviewed for this book. Recruited from outside YouTube, she acknowledges that the organization "up-leveled" the role from director level to CMO and VP because the business was evolving.

YouTube, a video-sharing website created by three former PayPal employees in 2005, was bought by Google for $1.65 billion in 2006, and now

1   IBM's State of Marketing Survey 2012—Marketers' biggest challenges and opportunities reveal the rise of the empowered customer. IBM Software Group. [Online, 2012]. Available at: http://www-01.ibm.com/software/marketing-solutions/campaigns/surveys/2012-marketers-survey.html [accessed November 25, 2012].

operates as a subsidiary of Google. As such, Tiedt has a dual reporting line to the CEO of YouTube as well as the CMO of Google, and she sits on the YouTube executive committee. Her role is not just B2C, but also B2B, and she splits her time roughly 50 percent on both.

She jumped into the role which she likens to "drinking by fire hose," and as she says, "I think most people in technology companies would tell you, there's not a very rigid or defined onboarding process. Onboarding is just kind of getting your hands on as much information as possible … And I had one-on-ones with every person on the team to get a sense of what's working, what's not working. And I had about 30 one-on-ones with other people throughout YouTube to understand where marketing has been, where marketing needs to go, and where does the business need to go."

Tiedt claims that 30 percent of her time has been spent keeping the trains running on the programs already in process, and the remaining 70 percent spent on learning as much as possible to enable her to pull together her own plan. And part of that was changing up the organization chart. She has some 55 individuals in her team, which includes six direct reports.

In terms of her responsibilities, Tiedt has marketing planning, advertising, media, partner communications, partner marketing, global regional marketing, editorial, analytics, product marketing, branding. "The only thing that isn't directly reporting in is PR which, at Google, sits as a separate function from marketing," she says. "But the nice thing is that they sit with us in the open floor plan, so from an integration standpoint, just the pure proximity of where we sit has been great."

In terms of B2B, she has a partner who is focused on selling to advertisers, but she also looks after B2B marketing for YouTube which is directed to developers, partners and content creators. Tiedt also manages Google TV marketing, so she works with OEM and distribution partners talking through matters such as how to get the YouTube application on Play Station, X-Box, phones, iPads, and so on.

While she has been getting to grips with the business, her responsibilities, and looking ahead, she is extremely positive about the YouTube culture. "I'm surprised at how helpful everyone wants to be in helping you succeed. I think I was a little surprised at that. I think that I thought I would be more on my own trying to get things done — there is no onboarding process, so you're just trying to figure it out. But I didn't expect there to be as much desire to help," she says.

Moving forward, Tiedt's priorities are focused on getting the organizational structure right: "I need to get people hired, I need to get the team re-orged — that needs to be the very top priority. Get the right team so that we're clear and we're set up for success. The next 90 days also includes 2013 planning — developing the plan that we feel comfortable executing on. So I want to move the team from, you know, the 100 priorities we have right now to four or five priorities and really get the team focusing on less is more ... and having strong business fundamentals backing up why those would be the big things that will impact the business."

Tiedt is a huge fan of data. "We've got a whole lot of data, but data in and of itself doesn't help you. You're really trying to distill it down to the three to five insights that you should be pivoting a plan off of, and as you peel back the onion, what's the center of that onion and what are the things that you need to care most about," she remarks. And she takes ownership of understanding that data. "It's less about hiring more data analysts; and it's more about needing to prioritize my own time to go through the data and come up with my own assumptions. Because five other people will have their own reads of the data, and we need to have the intellectual debate. I think that's where the right insights come out and I have to be informed enough about the data to be able to have a point of view," she reasons. "I think the intellectual debate is the most important part of the process."

Among her early wins, Tiedt lists where she and marketing are with the YouTube team: "Change is hard, and there could have been organ rejection," which she relates to her own appointment. "But I am proud that I feel like I have a good working relationship with my peers ... And I think that people are wanting to hear what my perspective is and what marketing's perspective is."

She also counts a culture of curiosity being built within the marketing discipline. "I think sometimes you need change in a new person coming in just to have a reason to start diving into the data and asking questions. And I'm starting to see people doing it now even without my prompting, which makes me real happy."

Macy's

MARTINE REARDON, CMO, MACY'S

 **Martine Reardon is CMO of Macy's. She has risen through the ranks at Federated Department Stores and Macy's Inc., beginning in the special events department at Abraham and Strauss, and becoming CMO after serving most recently as Macy's EVP of marketing and advertising. Under her leadership, Macy's has been named Mobile Marketer of the Year, received the Golden Halo Award for cause marketing, and scored a digital IQ of Genius in retail marketing.**

Martine Reardon joined Macy's Department Stores in 1995 when Federated Department Stores acquired Macy's. She had been at Abraham and Strauss which also was owned by Federated, and before becoming Macy's CMO in February 2012, she was EVP of marketing and advertising there. Becoming CMO, she joined the executive committee of the organization, and she now reports to the company's chief merchandising officer "because so much of what marketing does is market the products that we sell in our stores," she says.

Macy's is a US chain of mid-range to upscale department stores. In addition to its internationally renowned flagship Herald Square location in Manhattan, New York City, the company operates over 850 other stores in the US as of September 12, 2012. It has produced the annual, iconic Macy's Thanksgiving Day Parade New York City since 1924, and sponsored the City's annual Fourth of July fireworks display since 1976.

Reardon's responsibilities include advertising, creative development, social mobile and digital media, brand PR, cause and tourism marketing, special events, media planning, consumer insights and data analysis for its more than 800 stores nationwide. In addition, she helms Thanksgiving Day Parade, along with overseeing glamorous fashion shows, fireworks displays and flower shows around the country.

"It all starts with the product," she says. "The reason Macy's exists is because of the product. I like to think of marketing as the icing on the cake, sometimes the jelly in the donut. There's this sort of frame, but the real content and the real connection to the customer comes from the marketing arm. Today I'm really fortunate to own the customer relationship, whether it's through any communication in print, in digital, what the look and the feel of the brand is, actually, even the look and feel of the brand internally as well. We develop all of that."

With Reardon's promotion to CMO, there have been some subtle shifts to upshift the marketing efforts such as increased emphasis on technology. As she says, "We better be not only on trend, we better be ahead of it. That's where I work very, very closely with our chief intelligence officer, who leads our work in database and web presence.

Additionally, while she has been working with advertising agency JWT since 2005, there have been some changes and additions made to the team as the digital age has become a more important part of Macy's media mix. "There have been folks that have been sitting on the Macy's account since we started working together, but we've brought in some new faces in the last three months because we're always trying to keep things fresh with new ideas. At the same time, we want to make sure that we've got people on the business who really understand our brand."

Reardon also can boast of an in-house agency-type team in her overall group of 607 people. "Much of the ideas and the creative is truly a collaboration with the agency."

Within her team, she has eight direct reports with two additional dotted line reports. Direct reports head up:

- media relations, cause marketing and tourism marketing;

- parade and entertainment group;

- creative—print and digital;

- creative—television and brand integration;

- strategy, including analytics;

- research, including consumer insights;

- department operations, including production, trafficking and technology;

- merchandise marketing.

Dotted line reports include finance, and the Macys.com organization.

The tourism piece is a relatively unique element for a retailer. "This building [Macy's flagship store in Manhattan] still continues to be the halo effect for the entire brand because of the tourism just in New York. There's a very famous quote by Mayor Bloomberg: 'If you haven't seen Macy's, then you have not been to New York' because we are the number two tourist destination in New York, behind the Empire State Building. However I'm going to qualify this because this is how I always get myself in trouble. We're really the number three destination because the Statue of Liberty really gets brought into the conversation, except it sits in New Jersey."

Marketing is front and center in Macy's board meetings. According to Reardon, "Our board meets about four times a year, and then there's two smaller meetings. Marketing is probably on at least three of those agendas in some way, shape or form. Our board loves marketing. Our chairman loves marketing. Terry Lundren probably is one of the best CEOs when it comes to marketing. He makes himself available anytime we need him to be at one of our big events. He's at every single parade. He's at every single Fourth of July fireworks. We just took him to LA (Los Angeles) last week to do our big fashion fundraiser for HIV AIDS. He opens our events, and he closes them. He goes out and does all of our cause marketing initiatives. He really loves that side of the business. We're fortunate to have someone so supportive."

Nintendo

SCOTT MOFFITT, EVP, SALES AND MARKETING, NINTENDO NORTH AMERICA

Scott Moffitt joined Nintendo of America in May 2011 as EVP of sales and marketing across the US, Canada and Latin America. He joined from Henkel Consumer Goods, where for five years he was SVP and GM for the North American personal-care business including Dial, Right Guard, Tone and Pure & Natural. Moffitt's 20-plus years of leadership and marketing experience also include a formidable stint at PepsiCo.

Scott Moffitt joined Nintendo of America in May, 2011, where he oversees all sales and marketing activities for the company in the US, Canada and Latin America. Nintendo is a Japanese multinational consumer electronics company with its Americas headquarters in Redmond, Washington. Probably best known for its gaming devices, the company has created the Game Boy, Nintendo DS handheld video game system and Wii gaming system.

When Moffitt joined the company, the head of marketing position had been vacant for about six months, which was an issue given that there are so many interfaces between sales and marketing and the rest of the Nintendo organization. The first challenges he faced was the lack of presence in the day-to-day role for that period of time, and the cultural differences brought by Japanese ownership. "Different cross-cultural sensibilities are needed. There's a way of acting and responding that's unique. Every organization is unique. But I think you find from one US organization to another, maybe there are degrees of difference. This is one state of deviation beyond that," he says. **"Another thing that makes us different is that the organization has a lot of senior-tenured people who have been in the organization for a long time. That creates a stability and an inertia that can be change-resistant. So making change takes a little more time and patience. And you have to go about it the right way."**

And yet change is something which Moffitt is facing. "There are two kinds of change going on," he says. "And both of the changes are having a larger impact than I realized looking at it from the outside. The first change is that the video gaming business is not a really old business. The brands have been around for 25 years. So in comparison to many industries, this is a relatively young category, and the brands are relatively young. The industry goes through cycles based on hardware [game machines] being introduced."

According to Moffitt, the second driver of change is external. "There is a growing shift in the way consumers may acquire and choose to own video game products. And it's going from physical to digital. And the number of choices that a consumer has to consumer game content is exploding. There are ways that you can stream games to your home computer. You can play them via Facebook, on social gaming sites. You can play them on many new devices. So the number of competitors that are entering the space are growing rapidly. And this change in the form from physical to digital is not unlike what the book and the music business went through. So there are new competitors but also a change in form."

To tackle these challenges, Moffitt's responsibilities include:

- consumer marketing which includes advertising, experiential marketing, marketing partnerships;

- marketing, planning and operations—essentially market research and strategic planning;

- corporate affairs which includes public relations and analyst relations;

- entertainment trends which includes celebrity sponsors and entertainment marketing;

- direct consumer communications which includes email marketing, websites and marketing via the devices sold by Nintendo, as well as its own magazine, *Nintendo Power* Magazine.

Moffitt has nine direct reports including the heads of these groups as well as two reports in sales, and one report each in Canada and Latin America. Like Havaianas, Nintendo's product innovation is based outside the region, in this case, Japan.

An early win that Moffitt claims has been formalizing the organization's social media practices and processes within his first six months: "The gaming business has high, high, high consumer passion and involvement. It's beyond anything that I've been a part of. So we had many fan sites created on Facebook, but none of them were our own creation. So we wanted to use social media as a more active part of our marketing, so we embarked on a campaign to formalize those, to educate our parent company about social media, including our CEO, and we began merging these sites into a formal Nintendo-managed community. That was a big accomplishment. And now I think the whole organization embraces the value of social media."

Moffitt continues by speaking of the evolution: "It's changed our company in two dimensions. One is that we have gone from a one-way communicator to a two-way communicator. So we listen and respond as well as communicate out. And then we've also gone from a methodic marketing organization to an always-on marketing organization."

His second early win is a formally-articulated strategic plan. "We did not really have any written document that could be called the strategy ... now we have a business strategy." His third win has been creating greater cohesion among the team and stemming the departure of people which has been driven by the highly competitive talent marketplace, particularly in the Bay Area where there's a plethora of tech and start-up companies showering their employees with perks. Moffitt's team is based in the Bay Area as well as in Redmond and New York City. "What's challenging with running a team where you're in three different locations is that the competition for talent is different in all three areas. And the need to feel part of something is a human need that everyone needs to feel."

Vanguard

MIKE MA, HEAD OF RETAIL ADVERTISING AND PROSPECT MARKETING, VANGUARD

Mike Ma took on the role of head of retail advertising and prospect marketing for Vanguard's direct-to-investor business in June 2010. Previously, he was principal and chief business officer at kasina, the asset management industry's leading sales and marketing consulting firm. Before that, he held various roles in software start-ups at iPhrase Technologies (later acquired by IBM) and Trilogy Software.

Mike Ma was recruited from a boutique strategy consulting firm where Vanguard had been his client for eight years. According to Ma, his client said, "'We're looking for someone who knows digital marketing and understands the asset management industry and understands Vanguard's culture. Do you know anyone like that?' So we started a year-long song and dance about coming on, and I had a lot of misgivings—I'd been an entirely small company, start-up, entrepreneurial type of person."

Ma was hesitant to join what he calls a "big financial monolith out in the burbs of Philadelphia," but he believed in the company, he was ready for something new, and he was excited about the opportunity. "Vanguard had never done a major advertising campaign before, so I'm gonna get to be the chief story-teller for a brand I love that's never done it before? Sign me up," he said.

The Vanguard Group is an American investment management company based in Malvern, Pennsylvania. It has approximately $2 trillion in US mutual fund assets, offering index funds, active funds, electronic funds transfers (EFTs) and other financial products and services to retail and institutional investors in the US and abroad. Founder and former chairman John Bogle is credited with offering the first index fund available to individual investors, the popularization of index funds generally, and driving costs down across the mutual fund industry. Vanguard is owned by the funds themselves and, as a result, is owned by the investors in the funds.

As Ma says, "We're the world's largest financial co-op and we work to stay true to our core purpose of taking a stand for all investors, treating them fairl,y and them the best chance for investment success. Every time we make money, we drop fees. And it's something I believe in almost religiously. I've always recommended Vanguard."

Ma had worked with every B2B division of Vanguard, but his new role was with the "big, grand dame legacy part of the organization, the B2C part with which I'd never done any work," he said. While there had been marketers before Ma, the role was a new one with a new larger focus on incorporating advertising into marketing efforts.

Vanguard's client-centric, at-cost structure had a unique advertising consequence in terms of structure for Ma's team. "We run to advertising like it's a P&L. Every brick has to carry its weight from the funds we run, to the spoons we pick for our cafeterias, to our advertising in order to stay true to our purpose. We have to prove every single penny in advertising generates a positive return for our shareholders. Or we will just stop advertising."

Ma reports to one of the principles, Colin Kelton, at Vanguard who oversees retail marketing and communication. Kelton reports to the managing director, Mike Miller, who in turn reports to CEO Bill McNabb.

In terms of responsibilities, Ma has media and production matrixed into him since these functions are a central and shared resource with the B2B businesses. Retail advertising and prospect marketing is the biggest user of the firm's client integrated insights group which includes analytics, secondary and primary research. PR is a separate entity within planning and development, but he owns internal communications of advertising. Ma is concerned mainly with prospects, so social media also sits outside his team since that channel is reserved mainly for client communications, however he and the head of social are working more and more closely because, as he says, "We're like-minded and we know we can help each others' groups."

As Ma says, "My official title is senior manager, prospect marketing, which is equivalent to divisional CMO or SVP of advertising. But we have a unique culture." He makes the point that he's been brought in to change the course of the ship, but it takes a very long time. So he runs his team like a start-up within Vanguard.

Creatively, Ma claims, "Our successful delivery on the bottom line has enabled us to execute some creative ideas that are a bit unconventional for financial services. For example, we did this little promotion in New York, Boston and DC—the 'At-Cost Café.' The idea behind it was selling funds at one-fifth the cost. So people can smell, touch, taste and feel what it feels like to have a high-quality product at one-fifth the price. It was just a little food truck selling 28-cent cups of coffee—one-fifth the national average. It was a great promotion, and it got tons of awareness about who we are."

Ma has continued to try to teach Vanguard that it's okay to be creative. On a similar vein, he team created a promotion to communicate the investing message. Called "Vanguard at the Movies,"[2] three vignettes were produced around horror, drama and suspense—"Great for the movies; not so great for investing" and they were run via cinema advertising.

Creativity aside, Ma believes he's built credibility for himself and his team given his focus on the metrics and his understanding of the business. "This is where my background as a management consultant comes in. It's like 'wow, he's asking the right questions'."

---

2   *Vanguard at the Movies.* Vanguard Channel, YouTube. [Online, June 24, 2011]. http://www.youtube.com/watch?v=gEIqvSLBLvs&list=SPB5EF46976EA099C9&index=1 [accessed: November 27, 2012].

Travelers

LISA CAPUTO, EVP, MARKETING & COMMUNICATIONS, THE TRAVELERS COMPANIES, INC

Lisa Caputo assumed the role of EVP, Marketing & Communications for Travelers in June 2011. She joined from Citigroup where held a variety of senior management roles for over 11 years, including serving as EVP of global marketing and corporate affairs. Previous experience at Citi included serving as the company's first and only global CMO. Caputo created and was chairman and CEO for 10 years of Women & Co.

Lisa Caputo was recruited to Travelers by its chairman and CEO, Jay Fishman, with whom she had worked at Citigroup. "He's a brilliant businessman. He is strategic and focused. He is incredibly down to earth, cares deeply about his people and our customers, and has a profound sense of loyalty to the company and to the employees. And so the opportunity to work with Jay, combined with working for an iconic brand, is why I joined Travelers," she says.

Travelers is a leading provider of property casualty insurance for auto, home and business, offering its global customers a wide range of coverage, as well as risk management services. Travelers, which maintains executive offices in New York, Hartford, and St Paul, is the second largest writer of US commercial property casualty insurance and the third largest writer of US personal insurance through independent agents. A component of the Dow Jones Industrial Average, the company has representatives in every US state, plus operations in the UK, Canada, and Ireland, and also provides insurance products internationally through its operations at Lloyd's and in Brazil through a joint venture.

As EVP of marketing and communications, Caputo reports to two vice chairmen in the organization: vice chairman Doreen Spadorcia for marketing, and vice chairman Alan Schnitzer for communications. Her role was new since the functional areas for which she's responsible had never been together in one group.

Her responsibilities include marketing, advertising, media planning and buying, digital marketing, corporate communications—external, internal, and executive communications, creative services, research and competitive intelligence. "Philosophically, I believe in the integration across all these disciplines as well as integration with other functions. For example, there's a synergy between marketing and community relations and CSR," she says.

Caputo joined Travelers in June, 2011, and she sits of the management committee of the company, which is the top 24 people. She recalls that in her early days, she did a lot of listening, which is ongoing and constant. "I need to understand their [her peers'] businesses, what the levers are. And that's a continuous information gathering and educational process that I think is a must because yes, priorities change, but also you make adjustments to how you're running your business and I need to be aware of those elements in order to do my job effectively."

Caputo speaks highly of the culture: "My biggest and most pleasant surprise was the incredible collaborative nature of the culture. It is really unique and I think it's just an incredible testament to the people here. There's a lot of open dialogue, a lot of points of view given, which is fantastic. No one's considered right or wrong, but perspectives are really solicited and heard, and then when a decision is made, everybody goes in that direction."

Summary

Integration has played a major factor in each of the cases in this chapter, whether it has been about combining marketing with sales as in the case with Nintendo, or just merging a number of disparate marketing functions together under new leadership. And even where functions are separate, such as the case sometimes with the communications/PR discipline, there is a heavy dose of matrix working to ensure better integration across the channels.

8

The Evolutionary B2B CMO

Just as consumer-facing brand organizations are stepping up their marketing efforts, so too are those in the B2B world. And as each new CMO is appointed, they have the opportunity to update, change and revise how their companies go to market. Jonathan Becher of SAP sums it up best by speaking to two forces at work: "First of all, SAP is changing overall, and secondly, I believe that discipline in marketing, not just SAP, is also fundamentally changing. And those two coming together is why I think there is a fundamental transformation."

SAP

JONATHAN BECHER, CMO, SAP

 **Jonathan Becher was appointed CMO of SAP in April 2011. He joined the company during the 2007 acquisition of Pilot Software, where he was president and chief executive officer. Previously, he was CEO and president of Accrue Software—a publically traded website analytics company; and president, CEO, and co-founder of NeoVista Software—a pioneer in the predictive analytics and data mining markets.**

SAP is a global corporation that provides applications, analytics, mobile, cloud, and database and technology software solutions that help companies of all sizes improve customer and employee engagement, optimize resources, and orchestrate business networks. One of the largest software companies in the world, SAP operates in 120 countries, and Becher claims greater business growth than the sector.

Becher joined SAP during the 2007 acquisition of Pilot Software, where he was president and chief executive officer. He was appointed CMO in August, 2011, and he's the first to point out that he views himself as a business person first and a marketer second, having held three CEO positions in his career. "So I come with the mindset of what's the return on investment (ROI) for everything that we do. Or sometimes people like to use the term ROMI—return on marketing investment—rather than ROI … If you aren't prioritizing based on facts and if you're doing it based on guts, it's hard to defend your priorities."

"So one of the mantras," Becher continues, "is run marketing like a business, which means you need a formal strategy, which is part of the transformation. It means moving very much toward fact-based management and decision-making."

Becher is all about metrics, but he shies away from what he calls "ego metrics" that track activities or outputs such as how many people show up at events, or how many clicks on a website. "Those are the really big numbers that marketers love to talk about but they are not necessarily tied to any particular outcome that you're trying to achieve, nor can you describe their impact. So there's a wonderful phrase that I hear marketers say all of the time: 'What gets measured gets done.' And I think that sends the wrong signal. That causes people to measure all kinds of stuff that's not very important. So the phrase that I use is **'Not everything that can be counted counts; and not everything that counts can be counted'.**"

So how does Becher define the drivers of change at SAP? "So the SAP of the first 40 years is not the current SAP, nor the one we're going to be next. So that's one impetus to change. The second piece, which is at least as important, maybe frankly even more important, is that I believe that the discipline of marketing is under the most radical change it's ever been under … In the good old days, marketing was a lot about controlling the message. We would build message houses and word documents to say: 'these are the adjectives that describe what we're trying to get out.' Today, yes, we still create and amplify consistent and coherent messages, but we're also orchestrating a conversation that's happening among millions of people that we never meet. And we have to balance those two things."

Becher continues, "The second part of marketing is that there are all these channels of communication between a vendor and a consumer which are sometimes direct, sometimes social, sometimes through third parties, etc. And it's marketing's job to synchronize the experience so that no matter how you interact with a company, you have a coherent experience."

So how did Becher go about effecting change? "I believe it's not enough just to create a vision and a strategy; you have to focus on culture first. One of the quotes I like to use over and over again is **'Culture eats strategy for breakfast.'** And I think you actually have to have an aspirational mindset. For example, every leadership team meeting and every quarterly business review I have, I talk about three mantras:

1.   *'All brains on deck,'* which is a euphemistic way of saying 'think creatively not just about what your specific job is but how you can help marketing overall and the company itself.'

2.   *'From silos to teams,'* I inherited some excellent individual organizations, maybe even world class. But ones that rarely ever talk to each other. And turning the company and the group on its head to not talk about functional roles but unified goals has been very, very tough. One of the things that helped was aligned KPIs.

3.   *'Actions not words,'* which caused a bit of public compliance and private defiance, but it's all about creating a culture of accountability."

In terms of delivering against these mantras, Becher had a very long list of enablers, but one of the key ways he used to drive change revolved around a set of "10 KPIs that gear all of marketing thinking." See Figure 8.1. And he claims that, "If one fails, they all fail. It takes us all down. To use an analogy, we're only as strong as our weakest link now."

Becher says that the behavioral change has been incredibly positive. "If people see their colleagues struggling, they sometimes offer to divert resources and budget to help them out because it's good for them as well."

He also speaks to SAP's vibrant online marketing community. "Half of the marketing population is involved on a regular basis. There's always a core of people that post more often. We have a platform built on Jive that allows discussion between groups, and it really flattens the organization in a sense." In fact, Becher claims that SAP is the most social enterprise company on the planet. "I'm personally probably more engaged than I should be to be quite fair … And I do my own stunts. Nobody writes for me. This is me. I'm pretty active on Twitter as well."

SAP Marketing KPIs

Simplify Marketing	1.	ROMI (Revenue from MGO/Total Marketing Spend)
	2.	Conversion Ratio (MGO to Revenue)
Humanize the SAP Brand	3.	Audience engagement with SAP social communities
	4.	% SAP employees completing internal brand training
Invest in People	5.	% improvement in enthusiasm score
	6.	% of employees with development plan
Develop Pull Marketing	7.	% of booked and won MGOs coming from Pull tactics
	8.	Return on Interesting (Index)
Tighten Links to the Business	9.	% Growth in SSRS
	10.	SAP Marketing cost as a % of revenue (SSRS)

Figure 8.1   KPIs List

He continues, "My leadership team is mixed. Some of them are extraordinarily active. And some of them are a little bit less active. But by and large, we have some 40 approved corporate Twitter handles, 50 approved corporate Facebook pages, and I think more than 1,000 individual ones as well. We run 10–12 communities on LinkedIn. It's an important and growing channel of how we communicate with our audiences. But I want to focus on the word communicate because too many people use social media as a shouting platform and reward themselves on the number of Tweets or the number of posts on Facebook. That misses the point entirely. To us, it's a way of engaging in a dialogue. And I think one of the things that we're proud of the most is not how much we're interacting on third-party social media platforms, but how engaged we are in our own community. The SAP community network has roughly three million members now which includes customers, partners, analysts and SAP employees."

One aspect that Becher is particularly interested in is the "Idea Place" where anyone on the network can suggest a new feature that a SAP product should have or even a brand new product that should be created. The community vets it and votes on it. Becher says that since this was launched 18 months ago at the time that he came into the CMO role, more than 500 of those recommendations have ended up in SAP products.

While the overall scope of marketing hasn't changed much since Becher took on the role, the way it's organized internally has changed quite a bit. "But that's mostly to optimize things," he says. "As an example, social was in a different group than web, so we put those two functions together. Communities was in yet a third group, so we added that to the other two. The geographies were aligned differently than some of the sales guys, so we fixed that structure as well. So I would say we've optimized internally the marketing that changed the scope with one fundamental exception—PR and analyst relations (AR). And quite openly, the head of communications and I have been interviewed about this in the past. The two groups were not as well synchronized before he and I got our jobs. And I guess he got his job roughly three months before I got mine, so we both started at roughly the same time. And I'm actually quite proud of the strong alignment we have, not just between the two of us, but between the organizations to the point that we do joint planning and joint messaging. We can't do joint execution, of course, since we have different audiences. But we have synchronized execution."

Becher's team comprises some 1,400 people globally, with 10 direct reports. He says that SAP is a highly matrixed organization, so there are a number of other functions he influences or touches as well.

Although he was already at SAP when he took on his new role, Becher still managed to run into a couple of surprises. "There were less people in the overall marketing organization that understood the drivers of the overall SAP business than I had realized ... it was more endemic than I might have imagined ... The second thing is that we weren't as fully exploiting technology as some of the areas of business that I had run before. And there were opportunities to optimize, to frankly, drink SAP's own champagne because we are the number one applications vendor and that gave me some early wins."

Interestingly, Becher was interim CMO for his first three to four months. "The unexpected positive thing is that I didn't realize how strongly my former peers wanted me to get my job and almost seemed to run a campaign internally on my behalf to cement me getting the job."

Hitachi Data Systems

ASIM ZAHEER, SVP, WORLDWIDE MARKETING, HITACHI DATA SYSTEMS

Most recently VP of corporate and product marketing at HDS, Asim Zaheer assumed the role of SVP of worldwide marketing in early 2012. He has spent 20 years in the technology industry, serving in senior executive positions in marketing and product management at Compaq, Digital, and Archivas.

Like Becher, Asim Zaheer was elevated to the role of CMO from within his organization, Hitachi Data Systems (HDS), a company that provides mid-range and high-end storage systems, software and services. HDS is a wholly-owned subsidiary of Hitachi Ltd, and sells in more than 170 countries and regions.

"We're about a $4 billion plus corporation with our own profit and loss statement and so forth, even though we're part of the $100 billion conglomerate Hitachi," Zaheer says.

Before Zaheer took on the role of SVP of Worldwide Marketing—a newly-created role in the organization, he was VP of corporate and product marketing and the overall marketing responsibilities were split between himself and the VP of global and online marketing, which included field marketing.

According to Zaheer, HDS's senior management decided to consolidate all of the marketing under one leader. "One of my charters is to further the alignment between what corporate is working on and dreaming up in terms of global initiatives, our target market segments, our message to the market and so forth. And drive that much more in collaboration with our peers and our colleagues in the field to ensure that messaging gets into the programs that have been on the street," he says.

Zaheer oversees field, online, product solutions, marketing, global communications—which includes PR, media, analyst relations investor relations and internal communications, marketing, competitive intelligence, content management and publication, and analytics.

He has consolidated his team, from 14 direct reports he shared with the VP of global and online marketing down to six, and he and his team have built a social media center of expertise. He's also improving the quantifiable goals and metrics within the organization. "What I'm trying to do is have one set of very concise goals for the entire marketing or function so that we can measure on a quarterly basis, and revisit our progress against those goals by looking at very specific data."

"The good news," he says, "is that back in 2008, the company recognized that we had a weakness in marketing and we want marketing to raise its game, have a voice at the table. When I joined the company, marketing had a very poor perception internally. It was a company driven primarily by sales and by product management or development. And so what we've worked on over the last few years is getting the right talent in, as well as clarifying and simplifying our message to the market, and we've worked on social media. And then highlighting the fact that if you do this right, it can really have a positive impact on the business."

According to Zaheer, it has been a journey to establish credibility within the company. "Today, I would say that marketing is clearly a respected voice. We work collaboratively with our sales leadership, who to a large extent are our customers. And so that respect has been established. At the same time, we are establishing our credibility with the development side of the house, and we've tried to have data or information-based discussions rather than opinion-based discussions with product development."

Zaheer reports to the COO who is responsible for a number of key functions within the company and the day-to-day operations of Hitachi Data Systems.

"What's interesting," he says, "is that we're part of Hitachi and part of the Hitachi culture, so it's a conservative and to some extent consensus-based culture from Japan. And based on our success over the last few years, we've been asked to help our parent company how to market in other countries because Hitachi wants to globalize … I think one of the goals that I have going forward is to help Hitachi corporate understand the importance of marketing in the value chain and in the mix."

In terms of early wins, Zaheer points to a recent collaboration with the sales function—the company's global sales kick-off—which was staged in April 2012. "Our global sales kick-off is basically like a mega, giant trade show lasting three days. Preparation usually takes four months. It includes production of an event which has to be world class and extremely dazzling and awe-inspiring. And the content, including the presentations that the executives deliver, has to inspire the troops but also be tangible and credible and have enough meat to them to be relevant. So we're responsible for all of that as well as a couple of days of training the entire sales force." The 2012 event was attended by 3,000 employees from around the world.

Another early success for Zaheer is being invited to a leadership off-site by his peer who runs product development and product management, which to him, points to the credibility he's been able to establish for marketing. "Buy-in from that important part of our business is critical to our success," Zaheer enthuses, "And we had a great interactive session where they were very receptive to some things that we'd like to do."

While Zaheer is making strides internally championing marketing, he's also looking to create easily understood goals that are measurable on a regular basis, to articulate the impact of marketing to the rest of the company. He adds, "And after we have a few quarters of history under our belt, I want to use the data as a justification to make some investments in marketing."

Zaheer also is concerned with taking a more global approach, and not being too US-centric. "I challenged my team to come up with a new process, a new methodology to ensure that we have a global public relations plan going forward, and it's vetted by the geographies before we do anything," he says. He has also addressed the company's website which was mostly in American English. "We've had the website translated into a number of major languages including Spanish, Mandarin and French. A seemingly simple and obvious change, and not inexpensive to maintain, but has big ramifications locally."

HDS's regional marketing directors report into Zaheer, with dotted line reporting to their regional general managers which also helps to ensure a global outlook on marketing initiatives.

With greater global communications, Zaheer also espouses greater social communications. "We have a philosophy where we encourage everybody to be a social media ambassador … they can come to my organization to get the do's and don'ts and the basic tips on how to engage. We absolutely encourage our employees to get out there—they're an extension of the brand."

Zaheer also is planning to implement an incentive program for social where his team will devise a social media ambassador designation that an employee can earn, and even have on their business card. "Also, I want to develop metrics which measure level of activism in social media, and then I want to award a prize each quarter for someone who is the most active social media ambassador for that quarter."

HDS also has adopted the Jive enterprise social business software to facilitate internal discussions. "We've created a Jive community as a follow-on for my extended leadership meetings so that we can keep the dialogue going," he says.

Nielsen

MARCY SHINDER, HEAD OF GLOBAL MARKETING, NIELSEN

Marcy Shinder assumed the role of head of global marketing for Nielsen in September 2011. She's an 18 year veteran of American Express where she held a number of senior leadership posts globally, including as global head of marketing for Business Travel and more recently general manager for the Small Business division where she oversaw products as well as brand marketing for six years.

Unlike Becher and Zaheer, Marcy Shinder was an outside hire when she was appointed to the global information and measurement company Nielsen in September 2011.

The role was made for Shinder who said, "I really had set my sights about 10 years ago on being a CMO. I just was very deliberate about it. I started reading anything I could read about what it takes to become a CMO and I passed up promotions in order to take assignments that gave me the experience I thought I needed in order to be a CMO. I love marketing. It's what I'm passionate about and what I wanted to do everyday."

"I'd always been very deliberate about keeping a written career plan. And I had written my ideal job—it was CMO, not in media but close to media, global, B2B. Nielsen was perfect. And I just fell in love with the culture."

While Shinder inherited an existing marketing role, the position had been changed and elevated. "And before I started, I made sure to take a couple of weeks off to aggressively prepare so that I could hit the ground running."

Shinder created her "playbook" from her listening tour (see page 14). "What was obvious to me was one of the opportunities we had was to simplify how we presented ourselves. So I put together a very streamlined document and went back to the people I'd spoken with and said, 'Here's what I've heard. Does this sound right? I've heard that if we do these things, it's going to make a difference'."

Shinder's responsibilities include brand identity, messaging, sponsorship, industry relations, digital (web properties), advertising, research and metrics.

An early win for Shinder is the new brand identity. "We developed the new look, voice, and positioning internally, which is very exciting. We don't require a lot of outside agency support because we've built a high-functioning internal agency model." The new identity was launched at a large internal meeting in January 2013.

Leveraging assets is key, as is focus. Shinder explains this through Nielsen's digital presence: "We have a digital presence called Nielsen wire, which has around 80,000 followers on Twitter. And so we're constantly publishing off of Nielsen Wire, and we're looking to integrate it more deliberately with Nielsen. com. ... We try to be very controlled and then leverage a few assets well."

Summary

In all three of these cases—SAP, HDS and Nielsen—these newly-appointed CMOs have managed to elevate the marketing discipline within their organizations, and particularly within HDS, and improve the reputation of marketing. Much has been achieved through clearly-articulated and, in some cases, simpler goals and the addition of better metrics to measure success against these goals.

9

The Internationally-Expanding CMO

As market growth in the US has stagnated in recent years, with the developing countries accounting for faster growth rates, many companies are looking further afield to build business. The CMOs interviewed for this chapter represent brands that are either expanding into new markets, and/or companies looking to achieve increased efficiencies in marketing cross-border.

Target

JEFF JONES, EVP AND CMO, TARGET CORPORATION

Jeff Jones was appointed EVP and CMO of Target Corporation in April 2012. Most recently, he served as partner and president of McKinney, a Durham, NC-based advertising agency, and previously, he held several leadership positions at Gap, Inc., including serving as EVP and CMO.

Target's CMO, Jeff Jones, is an exception to the rule of the revolving door CMO. He already was mentioned in Chapter 1 (page 7) for being the third CMO in the company's 50-year history. And while he's relatively new to Target, appointed April 2012, he stepped into a well-oiled CMO role that didn't require a lot of transformation, although it had been vacant for a number of months. The biggest challenge on his horizon at the time of being interviewed was the hugely important holiday season, but also, the company's expansion into Canada in 2013. Target is second largest discount retailer in the US, behind Wal-Mart, and announced its plans to expand early 2011.

While Jones doesn't believe the vacancy in the CMO role affected anything materially, he focused on the priorities for the business as threefold: "One is state of the business, one is state of the guest—and guest is our word for consumer, and one is state of the team and relationships, which means both my own marketing team but also there's just such a connected sense of work across every organization at Target."

One of the reasons why Jones was so attracted to the role is that, "It's not just a marketing communications role. It's a true marketing role where we think about growth as the core role of marketing." As such, his responsibilities are vast. "We've got 16 core owned brands, 10 of which are billion-dollar brands in and of themselves, and that brand management responsibility is in marketing. All of guest insights, so everything you'd expect a robust insights and analytics measurement team to comprise is in marketing. Of course, all of the media components: paid, owned, earned and shared. The communications function, which includes all team member communications for about 372,000 team members, all investor relations, and crisis communications. Of course all pro-active PR as well. And then weekly ad capability, which is an incredible business driver for retailers. There are 23 different disciplines inside marketing at Target," he says.

Jones has six direct reports cascading to the full team of some 1,500, most of whom are based in Minneapolis, but the company has a PR swat team based in a few local geographies, as well as a couple of hundred people in Bangalore, India, doing web development and photographic services. And, according to Jones, "We have an absolute world class in-house creative team of a couple hundred people, and we also work with what we think are world-class agencies that are creative agencies, media agencies, PR agencies, event marketing agencies and digital agencies. We have a fairly robust stable of external partners that we work in conjunction with our in-house team."

Most would consider Target as an entirely B2C brand, but the company does operate in the B2B space as a writer of prescriptions in the pharmacy and healthcare services area, which in turn is marketed to potential business customers for their employees.

While Jones stepped into an existing and well-functioning role, he has made some changes to more effectively align the team and integrate across channels. "So, the team had been reorganized a few times in the last few years, and one of my big platforms here is really about the ecosystem thinking approach to modern marketing. And so we've realigned some activities to frankly just be more intuitive and to bring things together. So one example of that is around insights, where we have a guest insights group … And then we have an incredible media insights group … So I'm bringing those two things together so we have a more holistic view of the guest across everything."

Jones says his biggest challenge is just getting his head around what it means to try to steward a $70 billion brand with the number of stores and lines of business, which he claims is just a function of time and learning. "Think about this continuum—on one end is healthcare reform in prescriptions, and on the other end is Missoni and design partnerships. And literally everything else in between. And so, yes, the design partnerships [for which Target has become infamous], are a marketing function as well."

Regarding the design piece, Jones states, "Marketing drives what we could call the advance team to source and scout potential future design partnerships. That decision gets made jointly with merchandising because we have to operationalize the idea. But we, marketing, tend to be further ahead in trying to figure out who they might be."

Jones clearly articulates the company's business drivers—"We have to create traffic, we've got to deepen engagement, and we've got to strengthen the love for the brand," he says. And he has created a powerful peer network which he calls their "four legged stool," including himself, the chief merchant, the CIO and the head of stores. "The four of us are really doing everything possible to get to know each other and build an incredible relationship," he says.

So he's poised for the planned expansion into Canada. "Right off the bat the Canadian guest wants Target to be Target. They're very clear. They don't want a Canadian version of Target … So we're structured to make sure we give them the Target experience they expect," he explains. Structurally, Jones says that the company needs to allow the Canadian team to move fast because they're starting from scratch, but that the organization also needs to give them the backing that a $70 billion company can provide.

"And so," he says, "that means that we'll have new themes in Canada for merchandising, for marketing, for HR, for store operations, and yet the core functions that are about the people and serving a guest, will remain the same." Meanwhile, it's been very important to the company to hire Canadians to run the Canadian business.

Jones speaks highly about the internal engagement at Target. Speaking about employees, he says, "They are our biggest brand advocates and so communicating with them in as compelling a way as we communicate with our guests is very much a part of our focus." He views that evolution as residing in marketing, not in HR, and he's proud of the internal communications channels that exist, including Target's "Red Talk" digital channel.

In fact, Jones has championed digital competency in a significant way through reverse mentorship as well as creating a digital university where people are tested. "It's designed to be a fun, interactive experience to give people a sense of their digital competency, but allowing them to do it in a private way. And we're building curricula around the results," he states.

He adds, "The team has always been so creatively-oriented. So now we're looking at what it means to modernize marketing, building on a foundation. And to help people remember that marketing is a strategic function of the company."

Mahindra

SP SHUKLA, PRESIDENT, GROUP STRATEGY AND CHIEF BRAND OFFICER, MAHINDRA GROUP

SP Shukla is a member of the group executive board at Mahindra & Mahindra Limited, and as president, he is responsible for group strategy. He is also the chief brand officer for the Mahindra Group. Shukla also serves on the boards of several Mahindra Group companies in different sectors, and he also oversees cultural outreach programs. He is a recipient of many awards and recognitions in his field. He is also regularly invited to speak at the reputed academic and industry forums.

From expanding into Canada to being largely ubiquitous globally, the Mahindra Group appointed SP Shukla as its chief brand officer in 2012. He also is a member of the group executive board, president of Group Strategy, and a member of the Group's investment committee. He joined the organization in 2011.

Mahindra & Mahindra's global presence means you can find the company's vehicles on the roads—both paved and unpaved—in Australia, Europe, Latin America, Malaysia, South Africa, and of course its native India. The Mahindra Group overall operates across 18 sectors including automotive, aerospace, aftermarket, agribusiness, components, construction equipment, consulting services, defense, energy, farm equipment, finance and insurance, industrial equipment, information technology, leisure and hospitality, logistics, real estate, retail, and, most recently, two wheelers.

Shukla enjoys the story of Mahindra's history: "The Mahindra Group was founded in 1945 by two brothers, KC Mahindra and JC Mahindra, and soon thereafter India gained independence from British rule in 1947. Following the Great War, they [the company] made the best use of the opportunity. Initially the company was in steel trading, and then they very wisely selected second-hand Jeeps from the army and started selling those Jeeps in the interior of India for transportation because there not were not very good roads. Jeeps were ideal for the poor roads in rural and suburban areas. They also imported Jeeps and assembled them. KC Mahindra was a friend of Barney Roos, the inventor of the Jeep. From Jeeps, the company went into tractors and since then they never looked back. Today it is a $16 billion group with 18 businesses."

With such a diversified business, Shukla likens its corporate governance as a "federal structure" which operates like the federal structure in the US or in other countries like India which also have many states. This leads to autonomous working and empowered workers who take a justifiable pride in their business. And he says, "By global standards perhaps we are still a small corporation, but in India today, we are among the top five conglomerates, and in terms of integrity, professional empowerment, honesty, and ethics, we are rated number one in the country. And that is something in which we take a lot of pride."

Accordingly to Shukla, this culture came from the founding family, and is perpetuated by the current chairman and managing director, Annand

Mahindra, who did his MBA at Harvard University. Annand is the grandson of JC Mahindra, one of the two brothers who co-founded the company.

With the core values deeply embedded in the organization, Mahindra recently created a common theme across all of the company's businesses: "Mahindra builds three things: products, services and possibilities. We are many companies united by a common purpose—to enable people to Rise."[1]

The track record of the company over the last 20 years speaks for itself. With liberalization happening in India in the 1990s, Shukla says, "Things started happening fast." He continues, "We managed not only the opening up of the economy with grace and agility; but also we actually started growing rapidly after that. The moment liberalization happened, all the shackles which we had on the growth were off, and the growth rate has been fabulous. It's unbelievable. I'll give you round figures. In the last 10 years, and that roughly coincides with Annand's taking over as managing director, our revenue grew 10 times. Our profits grew 25 times. And our market cap grew 55 times. And I'm speaking in dollar terms."

Figure 9.1   Mahindra Rise Visual

Shukla has a broad remit within the Group. He manages the Group Strategy Office which consists of 10 distinct functions:

- Office of Strategy Management

- Corporate Brand Council

- Office of Chief Economist

---

1   *Mahindra & Mahindra*. [Online]. http://www.mahindra.com/Who-We-Are/Our-Purpose-and-Values [accessed November 21, 2012].

- Performance Monitoring Cell

- Rural Insights and Strategy Cell

- Center of Excellence for Innovation

- Office of Risk Management

- Africa Desk

- Sports Initiatives

- Cultural Outreach.

Out of the 10 functions, the Office of Strategic Management is responsible for the conduct of "war rooms," a concept pioneered by Mahindra Group. All 18 operating businesses present their three-year strategies in one-, two-, or three-day meetings which are attended by the chairman, group CFO, group strategy head (Shukla), and several other senior colleagues from HR, finance, accounts, IT, as well as of course the business company or sector team presenting. These meetings take place from mid-October through end-December. Then, strategy is not re-opened again for one year. Shukla says, "So they're left alone to operationalize the agreed strategy in peace. That is true empowerment."

These meetings are followed with "budget war rooms" in February and March which are a series of mostly half-day or one-day meetings which convert the agreed strategy into annual operating plans (AOPs) with quantified goals, Any developments in markets or regulations are taken into account which might have happened since the strategy war room.

Then, from July through September, the group conducts "operations war rooms" to discuss how the businesses are performing against the budgets, and any change in tactics that may be required. This is also where possible market expansion is discussed. For example, in the automotive and farm sector, Mahindra already is in the US, Australia, India, China and South Africa, but the group is looking to expand into Africa and Europe.

According to Shukla, these war rooms also provide platforms to discuss starting a new business. "We are starting new businesses all of the time. For example, Mahindra Partners, which is an incubation arm, ventured into solar energy in 2011.

As the group's chief brand officer, Shukla also is concerned with Mahindra's "group aspiration," and this endeavor came out of an annual meeting with the organization's top 500 executives. "We have an annual conference which is known at the 'blue chip conference' where we share our achievements, our learnings, our targets, and also the strategies with each other through a formal process of presentation. Otherwise, in a group so large, with 160,000 employees in over 100 countries, people would never know what's happening elsewhere. At our December 2011 meeting, Annand held a town hall, and he asked our executives what should be our aspiration for the next 10 years."

Some executives responded that Mahindra should be among the top 100 companies in the world. Some suggested that the business should grow from $15 billion to $100 billion. Others said that Mahindra should be the most respected company in India. Still others suggested that while Mahindra was already great in India, the company should aspire to be in the top 10 in the US. And others replied saying that the US is a tough market to crack, so why not become number one in emerging markets such as Africa. "An important facet of that discussion was that participants were not just concerned with what we become but how we get there—by helping people everywhere to rise. That is what motivated them," says Shukla.

"To cut a long story short," Shukla reasons, "at the end of the town hall meeting, the consensus was that we should set our sights on being in the top 50 most admired brands in the world. And the Group Strategy Office will orchestrate the broad strategy, the regional moves, and facilitate tactics which will of course be managed by the empowered operating companies ... We took stock of our current position and, with all humility, today we are in the top 500 globally. So we have a long and arduous way to go in a rather short timeframe of 10 years."

Shukla acknowledges that winning admiration is a tall order. But he also recognizes that this is important to its the Mahindra organization with revenues and market shares following as necessary to achieve but not paramount platforms on which to be counted in the top 50 most admired brands. He can point out numerous proof points behind Mahindra's 'Rise' movement which is based on the company's integrity, ethics and its give-back-to-the-community stance, such as the fact that Mahindra employees planted one million trees in 17 months under its Hariyali (green) initiative.

How does this play out in a market-by-market approach? Shukla and his colleagues are developing and facilitating brand-building activities and initiatives in key targeted markets. These initiatives are designed to resonate with the local communities as well as relate back in a relevant way to the Mahindra business in that geography.

Shukla gives an analogy with the land discoveries that took place in the fifteenth and sixteenth centuries. "Then, you could go out with a ship and discover the Americas or Australia. After the nineteenth century, it was no longer possible to discover continents, though islands still could be found. Now even tiny islands and coral reefs are mapped out through satellites. In a similar way, discovering new segments in mature product categories is increasingly difficult. Now you're going to target and capture a market segment which is like taking over an existing land. Go with a better product offer backed by superior fire power and better trained manpower and capture territory which is already there on the map," he says.

As a result, taking Mahindra global involves a different strategy than the single-product line approach of the past—fast-moving consumer goods (FMCG), computers, apparel, and so on. According to Shukla, "Today, we may have different product categories from Mahindra leading the entry into different parts of the world. Tractors in China and the US, SUVs in South Korea and Latin America, motorcycles in Europe or planes in Australia. And of course, IT in North America and Europe. The rest of the products and businesses may follow the initial entry of a lead product category."

Among the varied initiatives aimed at moving by stealth to enter a market, Shukla talks excitedly about Mahindra Racing headquartered in Italy and Switzerland: "We decided to start participating in motorcycle races because we have started manufacturing two-wheelers for the last three years. Last year (2012) we won the Constructor Trophy in Italy. In the 18 months we've been racing, we've grown our Facebook page to 600,000—it is the third largest sport site today in India. But our fan following is not confined to India. It is getting us wide recognition in Europe and beyond."

In Mumbai, Mahindra has been organizing blues festivals, a genre of music also popular in Houston and the southern US states. In North America, it participates in NASCAR, and it had earlier partnered with the NBA (National Basketball Association) and Celtic Club to promote respectively basketball and football in India. In Sri Lanka, Mahindra is establishing itself as a household name through its sponsorship of the national cricket league championship, which is telecast live in all cricket-loving nations, such as India, Pakistan, Bangladesh, Sri Lanka, Australia, New Zealand, UK, and the West Indies.

Mahindra also has been involved in many important business forums. Shukla himself often participates directly. "I was in the Bloomberg debate with the chairman of Exim Bank and former UK Prime Minister Gordon Brown at the World Economic Forum. My colleagues and I get to speak at the World Economic Forum and other such platforms, where Anand also is a sought-after speaker. Where we participate, in public debates and discussions, we do so at the senior most level," he says. Shukla is, in fact, passionate when he states, "We are firm believers and supporters of public–private partnership. It is not just good PR but part of our Rise philosophy to make a positive contribution to society and community wherever we operate."

It is worth noting that Mahindra was the first business group in India to voluntarily pledge 1 percent of its profits toward corporate social responsibility, which is an intrinsic part of its Rise philosophy.

Citi

MICHELLE PELUSO, GLOBAL CONSUMER CHIEF MARKETING AND INTERNET OFFICER, CITIGROUP

Michelle Peluso assumed the role of global consumer chief marketing and internet officer for Citigroup in 2009. Previously, she worked at Travelocity in a number of positions, as SVP of product strategy and distribution, COO, and CEO from 2003 to 2009. Peluso also has served as a White House Fellow and senior advisor to the Labor Secretary and worked as a case leader for The Boston Consulting Group.

While some companies are aiming to be more recognized as global and to expand into new territories, such as Mahindra and Target, Citicorp already has a big global footprint. Citi's Global Consumer Banking (GCB) serves more than 100 million clients in 40 countries, and is among the largest retail banks in the world. Primarily known as Citibank, it accounted for nearly 40 percent of total deposits and 50 percent of total revenues within Citicorp in 2011.

Michelle Peluso joined Citi on a part-time basis first, just after leaving Travelocity as its CEO and having her first child. She worked with the TCV—

Technology Crossover Ventures—Group two or three days a week in 2009, and as the year drew to a close, Citi courted her to make a full-time commitment.

Making her decision, she said, "I really enjoy things that give you a bit more space to think more creatively, to be a bit more bold, to challenge the status quo, and I really sensed in the senior leadership team at Citi a really impressive group of leaders that wanted to think differently. Secondly, I love the intersection of consumer, digital and marketing. There's just so many fascinating things happening, and so this was an opportunity to take a job that really hit the intersection of a lot of that. So you run the digital channels but also marketing, client experience and customer experience. Third, I just loved the global nature of Citi … And finally, I just started to love the people."

Peluso started as head of North America Internet Marketing, and then about nine months later, she was asked to take the global consumer chief marketing and internet officer role, which she did in September, 2010. Her mission was to steer Citi to a much more client-centric bank by becoming more digitally focused and to create a model where local, regional and global worked more effectively together. She reports to Manuel Medina-Mora, CEO of Global Consumer Banking and Chairman of Mexico and Latin America.

She spent her first 30 days listening, and she also thought about the right model for a global CMO. "Companies swing from this sort of centralization–decentralization gyration—back and forth. And a lot of CMOs build their organizations in sort of a hub-and-spoke way with the headquarters, in this case New York, as the hub, and the countries as the satellite spokes … I don't think that model works for a variety of reasons. One, I think it's really disempowering for the countries and regions. Secondly, I don't think the best work comes from New York. Third, personally, I don't lead like that. That's just not my leadership style … So I actually came in and recommended decentralizing the budget to the four superstar regional heads—now we have five—that match the regional heads … And in exchange, I wanted to create a real cabinet feel with that group. I wanted us to be together every week on video. I wanted us to travel as a group together each quarter to a different region. I wanted us to sign up for five to 10 things we wanted to accomplish globally. I wanted each of them to own one or two of those things, so distributed leadership beyond their regional day job. They had to own something for the rest of the world. I wanted to sort of remake the global marketing team itself and dissemble it effectively and have the global marketing leader here in New York, but have him staff in different regions so he would effectively get closer to the regions, so a small, lead team that supports our global priorities but which is distributed ... I wanted it to be real co-creation, not New York-driven."

In establishing this sort of structure, Peluso also sought to change the agency model accordingly. "So we work globally with different regions co-leading because it forces them to be much more connected as opposed to just listening to what New York wants," she reasons.

"It was a pretty big change in their world," she continues. "And those two things have helped me form relationships with the heads of the regions, the business leaders, the global business leaders, and I think the impact is a very tight-knit community that is doing more things globally in a much faster pace than we ever were."

On the digital side, Peluso has been focusing on getting leveraging the channel for the Citi consumer. "We've done doing a ton of things differently, from doing our work in a more agile fashion, the technology, and really transforming the way we work with our analytics and our contact management systems to the actual experience itself, to building out a web design usability team, and bringing all that work in-house, to not outsourcing it to agencies. There's been an enormous transformation on our digital side. And the nice thing is that we've gone from mediocre rankings to almost top rankings in the past two years in almost every third-party study. Same on our social side and social listening and servicing. So we've made a lot of progress," she claims.

Peluso's team is some 250 people in North America, which includes eight direct reports, but globally, she has 14 direct reports and a few hundred people more as part of the regional marketing teams. She says that she's beefed up her team in terms of digital marketing capabilities, and in terms of talent, she looks for people who are culturally agile, transparent, eager to learn, non-hierarchical and collaborative.

Her responsibilities include advertising, digital including online acquisition and social media, research and analytics, and design and brand. External and internal communications are not included but they work closely together.

On the analytics piece specifically, Peluso claims that Citi spends a tremendous amount in the space, but she has reoriented the function to be less of the historical reporting aspect and much more predictive analytics, much more web-based analytics. "We have invested quite a bit in the analytic environment in the digital space, in methodologies for measuring digital and predictive analysis."

Johnson & Johnson

Like Citi, Johnson & Johnson already are firmly established internationally. According to Michael Sneed, the company has 55 percent of its sales outside of the US and it sells in 195 countries. But he says, "When you're in corporate, you really do understand how much people are still wedded to the US. I've really tried to get people to start thinking globally. I always say, I think for any US corporation, if you are situated in the US and you've built your business on the US model, you start with a real competitive disadvantage. Just because the future is really outside of the US, or its outside of most developed markets today. We have to continue to push ourselves to be uncomfortable with that and to know that we have to take some risk in places where we're not going to be 100 percent comfortable, where we won't know all of the answers, where the model is probably not going to be the model that we've all grown to love."

Sneed said that one of the biggest surprises in taking on his new role was seeing that more work needs to be done in this area for J&J, especially at the overall corporate level: "I think it happens a lot more in the operating companies because they deal with it every day. But in corporate, I think that because we're somewhat more removed, we're not operating that way as much as we need to." He clearly sees this as a need, and a way that corporate can add more value to the enterprise.

Colgate–Palmolive

On the same scale as J&J, Colgate sells its products in 228 markets globally (see page 55), and Nigel Burton sees one of his challenges as achieving the right balance between top down and bottom up. "We think it's very hard to tell what people what to do from the center independent of the risks of being wrong — **one of my favorite expressions is 'There are no consumers on Park Avenue'**," he reasons. **"Maybe if your headquarters was in the Midwest, you could pretend to do global centralized innovation.** But I don't think a headquarters, and certainly one on Park Avenue [where Colgate is headquartered], is a great place to get things right. So independent of the fact that you might get it wrong, even if you were getting it right, it seems to me, and it seems to Colgate, to be very hard to tell people what to do as some of our competitors do and then expect to get results. Or more importantly, you have people who feel they're accountable for results."

"So we've always felt that it's very important, even though we give this appearance of being a very globally-run company, there is input and creation from a regional and sometimes even from a local country basis," he adds.

Summary

Whether CMOs are in geographically-expanding organizations or companies which already are multinational, there's another layer of complexity on top of the single-market demands. Establishing a brand in a new market, driving awareness, educating customers and employees alike about the product offering, and then finding the right balance between creating value from the center, sharing best practice and learning from the markets is indeed a tall order. And some companies are recognizing this by putting in place seasoned professionals who have strong operational experience as well as a passion for marketing, even as the discipline itself is morphing.

10

The Turn-Around CMO

In an environment where business models are continually shifting and, in some cases, becoming completely outdated and irrelevant, and where new business models are being created and launched regularly, strong marketers are often sought out as solutions—or at least part of a solution. Two such cases are detailed in this chapter where the appointment of a CMO has been sought by the CEO and the board as part of a business solution.

Gannett

MARYAM BANIKARIM, SVP AND CMO, GANNETT CORPORATION

In March 2011, Maryam Banikarim was named SVP and CMO of Gannett Co., Inc. Prior to joining Gannett, she served as SVP for integrated sales marketing at NBC Universal where she worked across the company's portfolio of content to develop custom, innovative marketing solutions on behalf of clients. Previously, she was the CMO of Univision Communications Inc., the premier Spanish-language media company in the US.

Maryam Banikarim was appointed SVP and CMO of Gannett Co., Inc., in March 2011. Gannett is the largest US newspaper publisher as measured by totally daily circulation. Known most notably as publisher of national newspaper *USA Today*, it also owns 82 local daily newspapers as well as 23 television stations through Gannett Broadcasting Inc. It is the largest owner of NBC-affiliated stations, and it also owns substantial properties in digital media.

When Banikarim was approached by Gannett, she had only just joined NBC Universal. "I didn't take the meeting as an interview. I took it as a favor for somebody who was doing consulting for them [Gannett]. I think they had an idea that a CMO would make a difference in their business. And they wanted to just get an outside perspective on something that they'd gotten recommendations on from a consultant. So I came to meet the CEO and the COO and said, 'Based on what you're saying, it sounds like this is probably a worthwhile direction.'... At the end of the conversation, they said, 'Would you consider the job?'"

This dance went on for a few months. Banikarim suggested people who would make good candidates. She explained that she didn't want to relocate from New York City to Tysons Corner, Virginia, where the company was headquartered. Meanwhile, the position remained vacant.

At the same time, Banikarim said, "When I took the job at NBC, I really thought that was going to be my dream job. I wasn't expecting the company to be put up for sale a year into my being there. Sometimes not everything lines up quite the way you think. I had just been through being acquired at Univision. I knew what the next few years would be like. And I talked to my 'kitchen cabinet.' People kept saying, 'That's a big job [at Gannett]. You don't get too many CMO jobs with a seat at the table where they're actually looking at marketing as a revenue driver, not just an expense line.' So there were a lot of things that were appealing. Probably my favorite class in business school was turn-arounds. And it's a big thing to try and turn around a company that's been around for 106 years. And being part of that team mattered. I really liked the management team. So there were a lot of things that were appealing."

With being courted by Gannett and NBC being put up for sale, Banikarim decided to join Gannett. It was a newly-created position—the first time Gannett had a CMO across all of its properties. According to Banikarim, "This was a company that had historically been decentralized. When you're trying to create connective tissue, you need some core capabilities at the center. And the two that they identified were digital and marketing."

"There was no big onboarding process," she says. "Oftentimes, in these jobs, it's a leap of faith ... **There's a job description, but you have to be good with gray areas. You have to be a self-starter. You have to be able to see the pieces and start making things happen. And as more things began to happen, more things got put into this job.**"

Since her appointment, Banikarim has been given increased responsibility. Initially, she inherited three people in corporate communications, some folks in graphics and audio video, and some research people—probably a total of 15 individuals. She quickly picked up responsibility for *USA Today*, which added another 60 people to her team. And more recently, she inherited the national sales team and function, which added another 150.

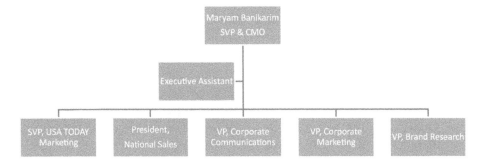

Figure 10.1   Gannett Organizational Chart

"When you're going through a turn-around or you're in a start-up, there are no lines," she states. "So when I recruit people, I say to them, 'If you like lines, this is your worst nightmare of a job. If you don't like lines, the opportunity is yours for the taking' ... The job morphs. When it doesn't exist, it evolves."

As an aside, Banikarim talks about being a parent: My worst experience in the playground is the swing. That repetitive motion, the back and forth—just lock me up and throw the key away ... And I think it's the same thing with the job. Most of my jobs have been undefined."

"You think a turn-around is hard from the outside. But it's really hard. Because it's a lot of moving pieces at the same time. So, somebody told me a term that I wasn't familiar with, which was 'whac-a-mole.' I run hard at my job. But the level of prioritization that's required—it's not like there's some things that aren't important. Everything becomes equally important. Do you work on employee morale and corporate culture over revenue? In a turn-around, that matters so much. But so does revenue."

In her first 30 days, Banikarim did a lot of listening. At the same time, she knew people were looking for results yesterday. "My job is really about supporting the CEO and putting her out there, doing her town hall, and working with investor relations on the first-ever investor day and things like that ... Part of your job is actually to be the greaser of the wheels," she says.

She's particularly proud of a purpose project she jump-started because "it was clear that morale was an issue, which is always the case in a turn-around."

According to Banikarim, "Morale was low, but they were very motivated. Nobody comes to work at Gannett for the money. So something else was motivating them. They wanted the company to win. They had stayed at Gannett for years, but people were dying for a sense of where we were going. Nobody had given them a path."

So Banikarim and her team did a lot of listening, and ultimately determined that people come to Gannett to work because they want to make a difference, and that, "Gannett is in the business of serving our communities, which is a much broader way of looking at the business. The language didn't come from us, the management, it came from the employees, which really made a difference. Especially since journalists are particularly skeptical as a breed," she reasons.

Concurrent to the development of the purpose project, Gannett had Boston Consulting Group (BCG) working with the management team on the turn-around strategy. Banikarim was concerned that BCG would see the purpose project as "fluffy." "They're [BCG] not fluffy," she said. When she presented the purpose project to the board as the over-arching strategy, which ultimately would inform business decisions, not surprisingly from her point of view, there was some dissent from the BCG team. But one of the board members was a senior marketer from Coca-Cola, who supported the purpose project wholeheartedly. Banikarim recalls, "It was really helpful to have a CMO on the board."

As a next phase, Gannett decided to host its first-ever investor day, and as Banikarim had already said, "There is no technical thing that isn't part of your job, so guess what, I ran the investor day. Again, not my job specifically. But somebody had to do it ... And we needed to unveil our strategy to Wall Street before we announced it to employees. With our morale issue, we needed to manage the communications very carefully."

Centralizing and tracking the marketing efforts across media channels—paid, owned and earned—has made a difference, too, according to Banikarim.

And from initially inheriting a digital PR agency, she has brought in additional partners to support her team including a strategy firm, investor relations firm, brand identity firm and a sports marketing agency.

Quiznos

SUSAN LINTONSMITH, GLOBAL CMO, QUIZNOS

Susan Lintonsmith was appointed global CMO for Quiznos in July 2012. She was formerly a business consultant with the Einstein Noah Restaurant Group. Prior to that, Lintonsmith was CMO at Red Robin Gourmet Burgers for nearly five years. She has also held senior positions with White Wave Foods (on Horizon Organic Dairy), Western Union, The Coca-Cola Company and Pizza Hut.

Like Banikarim, Susan Lintonsmith joined Quiznos as its CMO from the outside in July 2012. Quiznos is a franchised fast-food premium sub restaurant company based in Denver, Colorado. With some 4,000 restaurants, it is the second-largest submarine sandwich shop chain after Subway.

Like others interviewed, Lintonsmith started her onboarding process prior to her first day. She says, "I had an extensive interview process meeting with each of the board members, key members from the private equity firm. And once I'd accepted, I was actually on committee calls prior to even coming into the office for day one." Her interview process took over two months, and she visited several Quiznos and talked to employees and franchise owners prior to her taking the job.

In her last interview with the private equity firm, she was asked to come in with a presentation based on her limited knowledge and insights on what she would do. "I had to put a lot of thinking into the business prior to even starting … Some of that evolved since I've gotten here, but for the most part, I think that if I looked back, there were a couple of things in there that I'm actually doing."

In her early days, Lintonsmith said that one of the key things was to read extensively. "I got every single research study I could get my hands on, data, just really combing through that information. The second thing was to focus on the franchise system. It's almost 100 percent franchise, and it's the first time I've been in a system where there are so few company-owned restaurants." So she has spoken with key franchise operators, made store visits, and attended franchise meetings and calls.

On her first day on the job, she boarded a plane and headed to New York City for a board meeting that took place on her second day. On her third and fourth day, she teamed up with the COO and his regional operations director to tour restaurants on the East Coast, which helped her to get an even better understanding of the business as well as bond with her COO.

Lintonsmith has responsibility for all of the traditional marketing — including interactive — and research disciplines except communications. When the board made the decision to change out the CEO (see page 15), they also terminated Lintonsmith's number two person who had been the acting CMO for the past two years.

"It was good because it gave me a fresh start to be the leader. It was bad because I didn't know what I didn't know, and I assumed I'd have him and then suddenly he was gone because the departures were immediate. So for me, I sat down and met with every single person on my team, and I'm only talking about 15, but I spent at least an hour with each person. I analyzed the organizational chart. Then very quickly I saw some gaps as to what we needed to focus on so I did a slight realignment. I didn't lose anyone, but just wanted to structure the team a bit more behind where we needed to focus our efforts to try to turn this business around."

Lintonsmith's goals are clear — driving same store sales growth and focusing on the US business, building stronger relationships with the franchisees, and improving profitability. Although the US is Quiznos' largest single region, the company has a presence in Canada, Brazil, Mexico, the UK, Ireland, Singapore, the Middle East and a few other markets.

In addition to the traditional marketing disciplines, Lintonsmith has responsibility for strategic analysis and planning. She has been working with one of the agencies she inherited on the strategy piece, while at the same time assessing their capabilities. And she's looking at how marketing integration is delivered across the various channels. "Interactive marketing — social media, digital, the brand, website — is definitely owned by marketing. What's not sitting within marketing right now is the communications person and the way that we've used communications is more internally focused within the franchise system from a training and education perspective. I think an area of opportunity for us is consumer PR … It's a huge piece. Anymore PR and social are priceless disciplines with the highest ROIs."

Lintonsmith also is responsible for research and development and quality assurance, which, she says, means improving and maintaining product quality, new products and process improvements. "So, one of the things I'm focused on is putting a more disciplined process in place for new product or campaign launches."

Lintonsmith reports to the CEO and sits on an executive team together with the COO, the CFO, the chief legal officer, and the VP of HR.

Looking forward, Lintonsmith is leading a two-day planning off-site to develop a strategic plan for the business. "There's a financial plan in place, but I think that getting a strategic plan in place so that we're all aligned and focused is critical."

Last but by no means least. Lintonsmith said she's a "brand snob." "The other thing I felt was necessary to do immediately was to make sure the brand is really well-positioned." She covered this with the board about getting alignment behind the brand positioning "because I think it's critical to every decision you make from messaging to product development to food costs to everything."

How will all this get done? "You figure out the culture quickly and you think, ok, how pushy can I be?" she says. 'Figuring out the company, culture is key to knowing how much can I tell it exactly as it is versus sugarcoating it. And fortunately, I found the culture to be very straight-forward. My style fits very well here. I'm very direct so that has been one of those things that I've had to adjust a lot in the past. Here, it's okay.

Summary

Turn-around situations are clearly not for the faint at heart. Navigating an unclear job description or 'scope creep,' and creating short-term impact while at the same time creating an ambition for the longer term is probably more important in turn-arounds than in any other marketing situation. It's not a linear experience, and detours and road blocks can be many.

11

Partners in Crime

The people and teams with which the CMO surrounds him or herself are a critical component of their success. So much of what they do to steward a brand and a business is reliant on having the right talent, the right mindset and a passion for the business. That means that the marketing team, the marketer's peers and the marketer's agency partners all need to be aligned.

CMOs seem to be in agreement on the increasing challenge of finding good talent, particularly those with the right skills sets while at the same time culturally appropriate to their organizations. Getting the internal teams correctly balanced, augmenting existing talent with new needs in digital and analytics—whether that be through new people or training and development of current team members, and setting the right mission for the team, are key aspects of talent acquisition and retention.

In fact, according to a study produced jointly by Booz & Co, the Association of National Advertisers (ANA) and Korn/Ferry,[1] 75 percent of its CMO respondents reported seeking to develop new capabilities in-house, elevating the importance of finding and retaining the right people.

When Nigel Burton took on his new role at Colgate–Palmolive, he wanted to consider how the marketing team worldwide develops their core skills and capabilities, so he has been working on developing essentially what the requirements are, and building a clear set of competencies which will be rolled out in a training curriculum, building capabilities in a standardized way. "We'll look at talent from the point of view of career paths and succession planning to move people in a more logical way and relate it to the needs of the business, the needs of the function, and the needs of the individuals," he says.

Burton speaks to Colgate's history of moving people around, but explains that these moves weren't necessarily approached in a holistic way. "Now we're looking at it in the context of capabilities, competencies, training, career paths and succession planning … with the one caveat that mobility is now more restricted for two reasons. One, people are less mobile due to joint careers, family requirements, and so on. The second limitation or constraint is cost. It's actually very expensive now to move people around the world."

In addition to demonstrating leadership with the marketing team, the CMO needs to demonstrate leadership in the overall business, working with peers in the organization. Peers can be important because of the function they represent and/or because there are certain parallels to the CMO's role.

For example, Douwe Bergsma of Georgia–Pacific quickly identified that the connection to and integration with his counterpart in sales was a big opportunity. From a personal level, he joined the organization three years ago with a similar objective, to build capabilities in the sales area. "So, he was kind of my predecessor from a capability-building perspective. And he had the experience also coming from the outside, having a long career elsewhere coming in, building a capability center and then driving it in sales. And I was expected to do the same on the marketing side."

Given that Michael Sneed came to his new role from within J&J, he already knew the major players, but he also further developed relationships with his peers and would count the CFO, the CTO and the head of HR as critical partners. "I'm fortunate enough to have a good working relationship with the chairman and the rest of the executive committee. But what's been interesting is that in the role on the corporate side, I've been able to meet a lot of new people which I really didn't know particularly well outside of the US, so that's been fun. I think the one thing in a role like this is you know you're going to be forced to make a lot of decisions, so you want to make sure people understand that you're going to be fair, that you're going to try not to play favorites, but you're also going to really drive for alignment."

In most of the interviews, the CFO factored as one of the most important peers with whom the CMO should work and foster a relationship. Sneed commented, "The two most important people you should have are your CFO and your lawyer. The lawyer piece is a joke, but I would say that in J&J, your CFO is your most important ally. I've never been in a situation where I didn't feel that way. So what I found interesting when I got into this role was that because we had all these different functions, there was no one finance person overseeing it all. I just said that's not going to work for me. I can't do that. This needs to be consolidated. I need to have one CFO to handle everything. That, to me, was a no-brainer, and we made it happen very quickly."

In addition to managing down, up and across, CMOs are more thoughtful about their agency resources than ever before. Some have consolidated, creating a shorter roster of partners who have a more meaningful role to play on the business. Others are experimenting with small, nimble shops to test creativity and innovation, particularly in the integrated marketing space and as marketing relates to digital channels. Still some are not making any fundamental changes to their agency relationships, but agencies are reorganizing their own teams to create a greater sense of integration.

For example, Nigel Burton's team within the WPP Group announced in July 2012 that it would merge WPP resources and agency teams from across its network into one dedicated and exclusive team to work with Colgate. This team has re-branded as a single entity called Red Fuse Communications. The idea behind this? According to Burton, "We're hoping that we can develop bigger and better campaigns in real time or certainly in faster time because everybody's working at the same time on the same idea, or everybody's doing it at the same time. It's about being smarter and faster."

12

Creativity in the New CMO Context

Is data getting in creativity's way? According to CMOs, analytics are more important than ever. When John Kennedy, vice president of corporate marketing at IBM, spoke at a Conference Board master class for CMOs and aspiring CMOs[1] in November, 2012, he said, "By the year 2015, marketers will be literally contending with more data than astrophysicists. That's the scary bit. There's more data generated on this earth than the stars in the universe."

Kennedy also talked specifically about the concept of "big data" being more than just volume, but as well velocity, variety and varacity.

So how is this changing the marketing profession and specifically the creative output? While CMOs continue to invest in more insights and more talent to decipher the insights, just how much of the current fixation on data is affecting creativity?

According to Jeff Jones of Target, "One of the most interesting parts of my [job] interview, including from board directors, was understanding how I use intuition and how do I use data to make decisions. Not just are you comfortable with data, but are you comfortable following your gut? Because it's easy to say 'let's do that' but that often times requires more courage."

Jonathan Becher says, "There has been what I call the science of marketing. And there's been the art of marketing, if you'll allow me to be that pejorative for the two of them. But they rarely talked. And those two have to, as I sometimes say, get married. When they disagree, science informs art, and art trumps

---

1   November 8, 2012 Conference. *New/Next CMO: A Master Class for Current and Aspiring CMOs.* The Conference Board. [Online]. Available at: https://www.conference-board.org/conferences/conferencedetail.cfm?conferenceid=2414 [accessed: November 11, 2012].

science. But too often, they don't talk to each other at all. And there are lots of examples. Marketing is fundamentally changing. And if you don't change, honestly, I think you become extinct."

And another supporter of the marriage between art and science is Marc de Grandpre of KIND: "I think that gut's great, but you have to have some more actual data and I think that data has become our friend. It used to be a foe to a some extent and now I'm the first to say, if I can't get data or an ROI on this, I'm not sure—I still believe it's art and science, there's an art and science to it but we have enough resources to find the data to say this is working or not working. As long as you can see trends and build on trends, I think you can be very accountable for what you do and be very efficient in your marketing role."

In its fall CMO Club Thought Leadership Summit,[2] Danielle Tiedt of YouTube participated in a panel discussing the merits of data to creativity. She said, "There's a limit on what you can put out to test. At some point you have to make a gut call on whether it's good or not because you only have so many resources for creative expression. You need data, but you need your own creative instincts to come up with the right thing that solves the problem that you uncovered through the insights … There will always be art to marketing—always…"

Everyone seems to agree on the importance of having insights to inform strategy and creative thinking but creative testing is another thing altogether. As Tiedt responded, "There's nothing more controversial than creative testing." And on that same CMO Club panel, Christine Heckart from ServiceSource, expressed a particular dislike of focus groups: "Focus groups can be a very useful tool and they can be a really horrific tool, and it all depends on whether or not you're smart enough to ask the questions in the right way." And Tiedt and Heckart agree that "group think" in a focus group can ultimately re-engineer your story.

So just how much should CMOs rely on data as part of the creative process? The tension between data and creativity was and always is demonstrable at the annual Cannes Lions International Festival of Creativity held in June each year. At a panel held on the Festival "fringe" in 2012, it was debated at length as

---

2   October 5–6, 2011 Conference. *October CMO Thought Leadership Summit.* The CMO Club. [Online]. Available at: http://www.thecmoclub.com/pg/event_calendar/view/29622 [accessed: November 27, 2012].

covered by *The Holmes Report*.[3] "Sometimes we hear about work that everyone admires, and they never do consumer testing," said Michelle Klein, VP of global marketing, communications and digital at Smirnoff. "More often than not [research] ends up killing the magic, so you end up with dumbed-down ideas."

John Travis, VP of brand marketing at Adobe, which owns analytics company Omniture, presented a different view, touting data as their new best friend. "As a marketer, we have been able to learn what works best and justify what we are doing, which is always the marketer's dilemma."

The tit for tat continued with Wendy Clark, SVP of integrated marketing communications and capabilities at Coca-Cola. "It is not a proxy for our own decision-making," stated Clark. "We're actually not looking for more data; we are overwhelmed with data. Our challenge is processing that data and separating the wheat from the chaff and figuring out how to use it. Sometimes you get such a rush around data and ROI that we forget that as marketers, there's a talent what we bring—how you tell a story."

The Cannes panel also included Maryam Banikarim of Gannett who expressed yet another concern—another way to "kill work" is "through committee." The point Banikarim was making was that, "Everyone thinks they are a good marketer," so you need to understand how to navigate the politics of your organization and your board. "An idea can get killed no matter how good it is, based on the politics inside the organization," adds Banikarim noting that a company like Gannett, with plenty of journalists, poses particular problems. "There's a lot of skepticism of anything that looks like marketing."

Another barrier to creativity can be the size of the organization. On the main stage at Cannes in 2012, Marc Pritchard, global brand building officer of Procter & Gamble, remarked that size can stymie creative experimentation.

But creativity can come from anywhere. Caren Van Vuuren of Usablenet said, "I think you're living in a world of co-creation and so I think in the old world, you created this legacy of having a greater advertising campaign, or

---

3   Sudhaman, A. 2012. *Data, Politics and Fear: The Challenges Facing Today's Global Marketers*. [Online, June 24, 2012]. Available at: http://www.holmesreport.com/featurestories-info/12050/Data-Politics-And-Fear-The-Challenges-Facing-Todays-Global-Marketers.aspx [accessed: November 27, 2012].

better event—something that you pulled off. In the new world, little ideas and having lots of them is the currency of success."

Jeff Jones of Target, when comparing himself to his two "legendary" predecessors who "had amazing runs defining and fueling where this brand goes," says, "I think for me it's all about how do we bring the way that we connect with the world into a more modern, digitally savvy future while building on great creative thinking, great brave execution, great design leadership. So I think all of us will be viewed as risk takers, but just in different ways given the different stage of the brand."

The trick seems to be finding the right level of science versus art which will be part defined by the culture of the organization, its executive leadership's stance, the size of business, and its appetite for risk.

As Erin Nelson of Bazaarvoice said, "I think the most aesthetical marketers—the folks like the Steven Quinns [CMO of Wal-Mart] and the Beth Comstocks [CMO of General Electric]—are incredibly analytical and incredibly strategic and thoughtful. And, yeah, you know that we make great creative because you kind of have to, but that's just oxygen, and you better be able to do that."

13

Characteristics of Marketing Leadership

Key traits of true marketing leaders vary from the technical skills and knowledge to the psychological mindset and approach to the ability to coach and mentor. When asked what they thought about the key characteristics of marketing leadership, the CMOs interviewed for this book expressed a variety of answers, but those repeated most included strengths in communication and collaboration, the ability to be agile and flexible yet decisive, have a keen eye on understanding both the business and the customer, and have an innate curiosity.

According to a new study by Korn/Ferry, "learning agility" is the most important quality to look for in a CMO today, yet it is not a factor considered in the majority of promotion and hiring decisions. Specifically, nearly two-thirds (61 percent) of senior executives believe that learning agility is the most important attribute to consider when promoting senior marketing leaders, but only 19 percent of companies are testing candidates for it.

Caren Fleit of Korn/Ferry says that learning agility is defined as being more accurate than intellectual quotient (IQ), emotional quotient (EQ), and other well-known measures such as education level and leadership competencies. It is the willingness and ability to learn from experience and then apply those lessons to succeed in new situations[1] and according to research by Korn/Ferry it's a rare skill—only 15 percent of the workforce possess this attribute. The good news: the research indicates that CMOs disproportionately possess this attribute compared to their senior executive peers. The CMO role continues

---

1   Swisher, V. 2012. *Learning Agility: Where does Learning Agility come from?* Korn/Ferry Institute Blog. [Online, November 12, 2012]. Available at: http://www.kornferryinstitute.com/institute-blog/2012-11-12/learning-agility-where-does-learning-agility-come [accessed: November 27, 2012].

to change rapidly; their influence base is expanding and the ways companies engage with customers is continuously evolving. Increasingly, CMOs are tasked with driving transformation agendas that drive measurable business results.

Here's what the CMOs featured in this book had to say on the subject of marketing leadership qualities:

Jack Armstrong

"I guess there are a lot of people in BASF that are really right-brained or left-brained, but there are not too many that teeter on insanity in the middle, and I think I'm right there at the point. It's not only about awareness in the marketplace, but it's about the trust factor and innovation factor."

Douwe Bergsma

"Being an integrator would probably be number one. And I purposely start to talk about brand building within Georgia–Pacific instead of marketing because brand-building for me encompasses so much more. Building a brand includes PR, design, packaging and our efforts with the trade, and they all have to come together because the consumer is experiencing one brand. They don't care who's behind it and what function or what department. They experience the brand along the path to purchase. And for them, it's all one brand. And they look at their alternatives in the market place. Second is innovation. I think you develop a brand and the brand equity for the innovation you drive through the years. Third is very strong communication in the broadest sense of the word. And last but not least, everything stands or falls by the quality of implementation. So those are the four things that I would look for in any marketer."

Marc de Grandpre

"You have to be decisive; you'll have so many people pulling at you, looking to you for guidance, that you can't be ambivalent in your decision-making process. And on the flip side, you have to be somewhat of a chameleon, able to adjust to the changing dynamics of the tools and mediums we have to talk to consumers. But one thing that

remains constant, yet I think too many folks are trying to reinvent the funnel. The funnel is never going to change, but what tools we use to get that funnel to be efficient are constantly evolving at a speed that is break neck, and we as marketers need to be flexible and comfortable with saying, 'I screwed up, this doesn't work now so let's go here.' And one key thing I've stressed to all my teams is 'don't take yourself too seriously.' Not trying to be jack-of-all-trades and master of none for any leader in marketing is absolutely important. It's too easy to get caught up in the glitz and glamor of what could be when you lose focus of what needs to be. The other one on my list is removing yourself from what's right and wrong and really trying to put yourself in that consumer's shoes. You can have an opinion obviously. You can provide input based on experience, but at the end of the day, it comes down to who you're talking to and what works for them. And I'll tell you here, I've seen too many personal opinions drive decisions."

Scott Ballantyne

"You have to have a really healthy balance of analytics, consumer insights and creativity. And you have to be absolutely passionate beyond belief. Drink the Kool Aid. If you don't like it, don't stay. And you have to be the voice of the customer. It's not about you; it's about the consumers. So I ferociously defend that point of view in everything we do."

Erin Nelson

"Marketing leaders have got to be strategic thinkers because they're the ones that are thinking about where do we take this business and this brand. The second piece has got to be a tremendous amount of understanding and empathy with the markets that they serve so that they can really be the voice of the customers. That sounds so trite but it's important. Making sure that the organization is focused on what really matters. And then the third, which is newer, is we have got to be the ones that really make sense of all of these disparate frames of data. I especially think that's true on all of this new customer data that we've never had before. We always used to have customer relationship management (CRM) data and transactional data and demographic data. We are now in this era of big data—we've got social data, we've got engagement data, we have entirely new streams of insight that we've never had before. And we're the only people that are going to make any sense of that and enable companies to go drive big valuable decisions as a result. I think that marketers typically get a bad rap but every marketer I know actually is acutely

analytical. But I think most marketers get painted as, 'Yeah, the guys that always wear black and love to spend a lot of money on the Super Bowl'."

Ian Drew

"Can-do attitude, don't take no for an answer, making the impossible possible. Doing it within budget, doing it creatively."

Jonathan Becher

"Marketing is the great uniter in an organization. It is the one place where the distinctions between products and geographies and channels and solutions and industries disappear, and the power of the unified part of the company comes together. There's a joke that I used before I came to SAP that if you're a good marketer, you're essentially Switzerland. You're at war with nobody, and you hand out chocolates to make everybody happy. A good head of marking is someone who is also 'outside in' focused as opposed to 'inside out.' And where sales owns the customers, marketing owns the name, the market, the outside view. And if we can always bring that outside view to every conversation, we're doing our job."

Julie Woods–Moss

- *"Resilience: having a thick skin and resilience and not taking anything personally is a huge asset.*

- *You absolutely have to understand the business end to end.*

- *Numeric—you can't switch off when people start talking about gross margin, customer acquisition—you've got to be on it.*

- *You have to welcome creativity from anywhere. If you can be generous with your praise of others, you get a lot more inclusion than if you seek out the lights for yourself, because the CMOs are always in the lights."*

She also praises marketers who see the value of networking, and the value of being truly connected to the customer.

Carin Van Vuurin

"A marketing leader is someone who can go as comfortably from big picture to tactical execution. They need to be able to live very comfortably in both of those worlds, must have the capacity. It's a bit like the United Nations because all of the stakeholders need to be factored in, but somebody has to make the call. That sort of disruptive diplomat kind of quality I think is certainly there. I do believe that a marketing executive must be strategic at his or her core. Without that, progress cannot be achieved. Then I'm going to add this one thing because I really think this is important, and I spend a lot of time thinking about it. You meet people who say I'm the CMO of this and they don't come across as very accessible people. I think executives in the marketing role have to be imminently accessible. A great idea can come from anywhere, and if you're walking around in your ivory tower, you're going to be closed to that world of ideas and creativity. So I would say accessible and humble."

Asim Zaheer

"Number one: you have to be a really good collaborator. The reason I say that is because you have to bridge corporate being, the back office, research and development (R&D) and product development—you have to bridge that with sales, which is front office. And you have to be a really good negotiator. You have to be a really good listener. You have to be a really good communicator, so wrap it all up you have to be a good collaborator.

Number two: you have to be a very skilled communicator because your function, its charter, is basically to communicate to customers and sales people, to the world. You have to be able to crystallize a thought into a very crisp message. You have to be able to influence people, with a clear rationale. And you're going to be speaking to extremely diverse audiences.

Number three: innovation. I stress innovation a lot within my group. I reward people for innovation and for new ideas and new ways of doing things. I do not punish people for trying to be innovative and failing.

It's essential for us to continuously evolve. The market is changing extremely fast. The tools with which we work are changing the way in which our target customers buy and purchase is changing."

Jeff Jones

"You've got to have incredible business savvy, you've got to be equally adept with the CFO and the head merchant and the head creative. You've got to be able to keep doing what works, while at the same time you're figuring out what's next. In this culture especially, but I think it's true in general, you have to set a tone for what it means to work in a world of accountability and creativity. You don't get to pick one or the other. You've got to be contemporary in terms of what's happening in the world probably more so than your executive committee peer set."

Marcy Shinder

"Integrity is the number one quality. Vision is essential: certainly relationship skills and the ability to listen well. Self-confidence. You definitely have to be analytic enough. It was why I took a general management assignment when I was at Amex because it was just heavy duty; no creative; it was all left brain. It was just numbers, analytics, P&L.

One thing for a CMO is how do you look around the corner? How do you see around the corner? And how do you innovate? Those are the key things. So how does a CMO get themselves into the driver's seat with the leadership of the organization to make sure that they're really inspiring the leadership not only to see trends but also how to think innovatively. And to really think differently and question convention.

The networking piece is something else I think is important. It's not my job; it's part of my personal time. And it pays off so much. It really helps me to think outside the box and help me to not just get caught up in my own world view."

Susan Lintonsmith

"The ability to be able to set a strategy—being able to take a bunch of data and make sense of it. The second thing I think is being able to influence not only leadership but in my case influencing franchisees. The third thing I think is communication. It's so critical in a multi-franchise operation. No matter where I've been, to have really strong communication with the executive team, with my marketing team, with the employees inside the building and then all of the retail outlets. In this case, all of our franchisees and their members—so clear and consistent communications is huge."

Michelle Peluso

"You have to be a business thinker. You earn a seat at the table. If you're a great business thinker and you create impact, the seat's at the table. CMOs who are too academic or too creative lose power quickly in an organization. Secondly, if you're not a consumer-centric and truly digital person, it's really hard to be a great CMO just because that is the value that a CMO brings to the table in many cases—being closest to the customer and understanding the digital interaction with the customer. Brands are so much less broadcast and hierarchical, so if you don't have that, it's a real problem.

Also, the whole planning process is changing rapidly. Agility becomes increasingly important. The notion of sitting down today and planning the entire marketing calendar for next year doesn't work anymore. It's iterative—the idea of agile, which is sort of a development methodology.

The last thing is just that passion for team building. It's just leadership—influence and collaboration, that is I think more important in the CMO role. When you're sitting between all of the geographies, all of the businesses, all of the functions, you're sort of the glue for the customer. You bring it all together for the customer."

Danielle Tiedt

"One is cross-functional stakeholder management. That's a really important one. And analytical skills is really important, not that you have to be a data miner, but you are able to think analytically and ask the right questions, and understand good analysis when you see it and shoddy analysis when you see it. Also a hunger for learning is critical. I think taste is critical. Not that you have to be the creative genius yourself, but you just have to have a gut for what's gonna land and what's not gonna land. Just taste. Not tacky. And I think good people skills is critical—super critical. I think the ability to motivate people, being the cheerleader for your product and your team—spiritual leader if you well. And yeah, good communicator."

Martine Reardon

"Here's the thing that I probably wouldn't have said three or four years ago: I'd say curiosity has to be the biggest one because with how fast our worlds are changing that if you don't stay curious about what's next and what's interesting, because it comes back

to the consumer—whatever she finds interesting or the latest trend. If marketers can be ahead of that or introduce those trends to the consumer, I think that's what truly is one of the most important characteristics to have.

Also collaboration because you cannot get this job done alone. There are so many aspects to the marketing function that you have to be willing to collaborate with all sorts of people...

It never feels like a job for me. It feels like it's just who I am and what I do and how I apply that. You really just have to have such passion. If you've got that and then you are smart enough to pick the right people to work for you ... It's really about the level of folks in the team that really make you a good CMO."

Carlos Zepeda

"Firstly, leaders and organizations that foster intellectual curiosity actually are able to identify better ideas. Leaders also need to teach the people to cope with change better. Second, which is related, marketing used to be very planned. You plan this, you book it, make a commitment, lock it up, present the plan and go execute it. Very sequential. Now everything changes, quickly. You need to be a truly real-time worker versus just a brilliant strategist and then a flawless executor. Being able to identify an opportunity on the fly and to make it happen quickly is critical. Third, you need to connect with your team, which is probably the most important. You need to be transparent and collaborative."

Scott Moffitt

"I'd say first, consumer curiosity or a passion for the consumer. You've got to want to understand how they think, what matters to them, how their lives are changing. And you've got to be able to take that information and apply it to your business or your communications. You've got to be restless about improving what you're offering, and that can be just updating graphics, being on the watch for opportunities for innovation, how you can extend your brand or have your brand meet more of their needs because consumers' needs are not static. They evolve and they change as they go through life stages or as they go through societal changes. You've got to be comfortable with and curious about the numbers. I've always been a very ROI-oriented marketer, and that's kind of why I've loved to have sales as part of my responsibilities.

Marketing doesn't work unless, at its core, it creates demand. And so your job is creating demand. And if you're not measuring whether you're creating demand, if you're not seeing it in the numbers, you've got to do something different.

And finally, a critical dimension is looking for good people. I want people on my team that are going to take initiative, try and make things better."

Mike Ma

Vision. Story-telling. And you need to be technically facile. You need to know enough about IT that you can build respect. You need to know enough about creative to build respect. You need vision and story-telling. And in a highly collaborative matrixed environment, you need to have techno understanding and respect for your collaborating partners."

Lisa Caputo

"Metrics is definitely one. That you want to have your performance indicators and you want to know how you're measuring your programs and making sure you're getting the ROI. And second is an understanding of the digital landscape and how do you position that company in the digital landscape, both from a social media marketing and digital marketing standpoint, but also a reputational standpoint. And how do you attract new customers and how do you retain customers, within that new channel. Third is the integration of the function. The functions should integrate and not silo, because when they integrate, they can deliver so much more value and there's more power in the integration in terms of value delivered both to the corporate entity but also to the lines of business."

Maryam Banikarim

"Learning agility...as defined by Korn Ferry...To be self-reflective, and make unique connections and see patterns that others don't. I think to be very open to feedback, and to seek new challenges."

14

What's Next?

What attributes should we be looking for in the next generation of CMOs? While the marketing leadership qualities in the previous chapter is a good place to start, can we be somewhat predictive of the future?

According to Caren Fleit of Korn/Ferry, there are a number of changes taking place in terms of CMO searches. "CMO roles are changing, particularly in industries where marketing hasn't been a core competency. It's becoming increasingly important, in many cases because companies recognize that they need to grab [market] share or add value to create growth. They need 'real' marketing, not just marketing communications but strategic marketing."

To quote the Booz & Co | ANA | Korn/Ferry study,[1] "Marketers tell us they are adopting a more collaborative approach to core marketing functions to ensure that they leverage multiple channels and skills sets. They are becoming more strategic about their marketing agenda, aligning it with the company's overall goals. Marketing is becoming more accountable by proving marketing returns through the use of data. Finally, the respondents said they were stepping up their efforts to play a more integrative role across business units and product lines to strengthen the effectiveness and quality of their marketing efforts."

Specifically, the key competencies of the CMO can best be illustrated from summarizing the content from a white paper produced by Korn/Ferry entitled "The Transformative CMO—Leadership Competencies Required for Success." See Figure 14.1 overleaf.[2]

---

1   Pandit, Y., Ripsam, T. 2011. A *Marketing Identity Check: Differentiated Capabilities Earn the 'Right to Win'*. [Online, October 12, 2011]. Available at: http://www.booz.com/global/home/what_we_think/reports_and_white_papers/ic-display/49841949 [accessed: November 28, 2012].

2   Fleit, C., Morel-Curran, B. 2012. *The Transformative CMO: Three must-have competencies to meet the growing demands placed on marketing leaders*. Korn/Ferry International Report. [Online, March 2012]. Available at: http://kornferryinstitute.com/sites/all/files//documents/briefings-magazine-

Key competencies

Skills Set

- Understanding the business
- Making complex decisions
- Creating the new and the different
- Keeping on point
- Getting organized
- Getting work done through others
- Managing work process
- Dealing with trouble
- Evaluating & deploying people accurately
- Focusing on actions & outcomes

Mind Set

- Demonstrating learning agility
- Being organizationally savvy
- Communicating effectively
- Managing up
- Relating skills
- Caring about others
- Managing diverse relationships
- Inspiring others
- Acting with honor & character
- Being open and receptive
- Demonstrating personal flexibility

Source: "The Transformative CMO – Leadership Competencies Required for Success", Korn/Ferry International, November 8, 2012

Figure 14.1   Key Competencies

When one examines what the CMOs who were interviewed "own" in terms of responsibilities and disciplines, and what's effectively "up for grabs," one can begin to draw some conclusions on the future remit of a CMO (see Figure 14.2, compiled from interviewee responses with the author).

Of course, there is no standard job specification for the role of CMO—nor even agreement on the title at times. Rather each organization needs to tailor its remit to its unique strategy, its business, industry sector and positioning in the market.

One thing to consider though is yet another finding from the Booz & Co|ANA|Korn/Ferry study which found that "the top 20 percent of senior marketing leaders differ markedly from their less successful peers when it comes to their overall 'emotional maturity.' They are noticeably more comfortable dealing with change and uncertainty, and they can address unpredictable situations without stress. They keep calm and collected under challenging circumstances without being aloof or too distant. They 'read the

download/The%20transformative%20CMO%20Three%20musthave%20competencies%20to%20meet%20the%20growing%20demands%20placed%20on%20marketing%20leaders.pdf [accessed: November 8, 2012].

Standard (Most CMOs owned these)	Shifting (approx 50% CMOs owned these)	Outliers (Only a few CMOs owned these)
• Analytics – insights and metrics • Advertising • Brand • Competitive intelligence • Business development • Design • Experiential • Field marketing • Integration • Marketing automation • Media (traditional and digital including social) • Partner marketing • Promotion • Shopper marketing • Special events • Sponsorship • Strategic planning	• Analyst relations • Communications/PR • Crisis communications • Demand generation • e-Commerce • Internal comms • Investor relations • Training – particularly in the area of digital/social	• Corporate communications • Corporate philanthropy • Design partnerships • Executive communication • Meeting planning • Packaging • Public affairs • Sales

Figure 14.2   Standard, Shifting and Outlier Chart

room' and can anticipate others' reactions; they can size up others and deal with social nuance."

This sort of emotional maturity increasingly will be required to address the sensitive balance that the CMO role requires. Extrapolating some of the content of Rob Malcolm's presentation at The Conference Board's "New/Next CMO Master Class," Figure 14.3 overleaf best sums up managing the tensions between now and the future, and balancing the differences between what stays the same and what has changed and continues to change.

Deciding the precise role of the CMO is just the start as well. It's important also to consider the overall function within the organization, and the sort of team and capabilities that can deliver against the need.

According to Mhairi McEwan, co-founder and CEO of Brand Learning, a consultancy specializing in transforming marketing capabilities, "One of the first questions we ask is 'what is the vision for marketing? What is its role in terms of what it needs to deliver? And is that aligned across the CEO and with the other functions?' We then consider what the business is trying to

Balancing the role

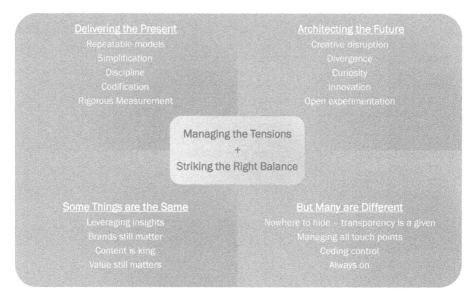

Figure 14.3   Balancing the Role

achieve. And therefore, marketing's role is in that. We will look at things like the organization structure, roles and responsibilities, clarity of global versus regional versus local, who does what. That is a massive complexity for many organizations and not to be underestimated. We look at the people. We look at working with HR in terms of attraction, recruitment, motivation, development of people. We look at the skills programs and what skills are needed."

McEwan points out that the process is pretty tough given that this sort of work is being done in a competitive context, in a very fast-moving environment, and in some cases, across a global platform.

Evolving CMO Responsibilities

When John Kennedy of IBM spoke at The Conference Board's "New/Next CMO Master Class,"[3] he outlined three imperatives for a new profession, which can best be summed up in Table 14.1. Coming from IBM, these aspects

---

3   November 8, 2012 Conference. *New/Next CMO: A Master Class for Current and Aspiring CMOs.* The Conference Board. [Online]. Available at: https://www.conference-board.org/conferences/conferencedetail.cfm?conferenceid=2414 [accessed: November 11, 2012].

Table 14.1   Three Imperatives for a New Profession

Three Imperatives for a new profession	How they change moving forward	How they translate into approaches
1. Marketers have always been responsible for knowing the customer.	Understanding each customer as an individual.	Interactions are so highly instrumented and so highly digitized so that touch points can collect a range of data, e.g. transaction data, interaction data, individual data, professional data. So, how do you apply sophisticated analytics to this body of data to be more predictive?
2. Marketers have always been responsible for defining what to market and how to market.	Creating a "system of engagement" that maximizes value creation at every touch.	How do you create an approach for every individual at every touch, e.g. offer, product, knowledge, advice, network. And how will you do this at scale?
3. Marketers have always protected the brand promise.	Designing your culture and brand so they are authentically one (transparency).	Culture is what people do when we're not looking. Transparency and authenticity has to become a part of defining your corporate character.

of the role not surprisingly are data-oriented, but given that analytics is such an increasingly important part of the role, the future of data is worth examining. And one of the more sobering statistics that IBM quoted in July, 2012, was that by 2017, CMOs will spend more on IT than CIOs.

The General Leadership Challenge

Finally, given the dual challenge of general leadership and marketing leadership highlighted in the Introduction (see page 3), it's interesting to note that one-quarter of the CMOs interviewed for this book had operational experience at the CEO or business unit (BU) leadership level. And CMOs have increasingly gone on to run companies—to name a few: Phil Donne, formerly a regional CMO of Kellogg's now president of Campbell's Canada; Marc Lefar, former Cingular CMO now CEO of Vonage; Richard Dickson former Mattel CMO now president and CEO of Jones Apparel Group; Pekka Rantala, former Nokia CMO now group president and CEO of Fazer; Keith Levy, former Anheuser–Busch CMO now president of Royan Canin; Martin Glenn, former Walkers

Snack Foods (Frito-Lay's UK division) now CEO United Biscuits in the UK; and the list goes on.

There's no denying that marketing is becoming a more integral and strategic contributor to business growth and therefore success, and yet, marketing remains under-represented on boards with the exception of companies that are highly consumer-marketing focused, such as retail operations and consumer packaged goods brands.

What will the future hold? Where marketing will be in the next five to 10 years is difficult to predict—so much more so than the roles of CFO or even the CEO, even though both are undergoing some transformation as well. But it's fair to consider that marketing will probably change the most, at an accelerating pace.

Appendix

Asim Zaheer, SVP, Worldwide Marketing, Hitachi Data Systems

Carin Van Vuurin, CMO, Usablenet

Carlos Zepeda, VP, Marketing, Alpargatas USA/Havaianas

Christine Heckart, CMO, ServiceSource

Danielle Tiedt, CMO, YouTube

Douwe Bergsma, CMO, Georgia–Pacific

Elisa Steele, CMO Skype, and CVP, Marketing, Microsoft

Erin Nelson, CMO, Bazaarvoice

Ian Drew, EVP, Marketing and Business Development, ARM

Jack Armstrong, Director, Marketing Communications North America, BASF

Jeff Jones, EVP and CMO, Target Corporation

Jonathan Becher, CMO, SAP

Julie Woods–Moss, CMO, Tata Communications

Lisa Caputo, EVP, Marketing & Communications, The Travelers Companies

Marc de Grandpre, Head of Marketing, KIND Snacks

Marcy Shinder, Head of Global Marketing, Nielsen

Martine Reardon, CMO, Macy's

Maryam Banikarim, SVP and CMO, Gannett Corporation

Michael Sneed, VP, Global Corporate Affairs, Johnson & Johnson

Michelle Peluso, Global Consumer Chief Marketing and Internet Officer, Citigroup

Mike Ma, Head of Retail Advertising and Prospect Marketing, Vanguard

Nigel Burton, CMO, Colgate-Palmolive

Scott Moffitt, EVP, Sales and Marketing, Nintendo North America

Scott Ballantyne, Global CMO, Fab.com

SP Shukla, President, Group Strategy, and Chief Brand Officer, Mahindra Group

Susan Lintonsmith, Global CMO, Quiznos

Epilogue

Given Spencer Stuart's research on CMO tenure (see page 6 — Table 1.1), it's safe to assume that CMOs move around more quickly than other C-level executives. Even though the average has increased from a recorded low of just under two years (23.2 months in 2006), to well over three years (43 months in 2011), the marketing community is accustomed to hearing about frequent moves of their peers.

So it should be no surprise to report that within less than six months of writing this book, four out of the 26 CMOs interviewed have moved on or moved out of their organizations.

- Michelle Peluso, global consumer chief marketing and internet officer at Citigroup, left to become CEO of Gilt, where she has served on its board of directors since October 2009. Her move was announced in December 2012 and she took up the reins of Gilt at the end of February 2013. The announcement of her move came relatively shortly after the resignation of CEO Vikram Pandit on October 16, 2012. She joined Citigroup in 2009.

- Mike Ma, head of retail advertising and prospect marketing at Vanguard, left to join financial investment start-up Betterment as its "chief growth (marketing) officer". He was in the Vanguard role for two years and eight months.

- Erin Nelson, CMO at Bazaarvoice, left the organization after two years and two months to become CEO of Bloom Ventures, a firm she launched in January 2013 to grow businesses, brands, and ideas through a combination of consulting, capital, and capability delivery. In March 2013, she took up the reins as President of Dachis Group, a leader in data driven social marketing solutions. In her new role, Nelson will lead Dachis Group's end-to-end go-to-market strategy and execution.

- With less than one year as Fab.com, CMO Scott Ballantyne left the organization. He joined Backcountry.com as CMO in March, 2013. Based in Park City, Utah, in the US, Backcountry claims to be the online specialty retailer for the great outdoors.

It's not unusual, as well, for CMOs to be given additional responsibilities within their organizations. One such example is SP Shukla. In early April 2013, the $15.9 billion Mahindra Group has announced that Shukla is to head Mahindra Defence Systems, a wholly-owned subsidiary. Shukla, who earlier headed the group's strategy function, has been redesignated as President, Group Strategy, Defence Sector and Chief Brand Officer.

Index